FLORISTS' REVIEW

101

one-hundred-one

SILK&
DRIED
DESIGNS

PUBLISHER:	Frances Dudley
ASSOCIATE PUBLISHER:	Talmage McLaurin, AIFD
AUTHOR:	Shelley Urban
COPY EDITORS:	David L. Coake
	Kelsey E. Smith
PHOTOGRAPHER:	Stephen Smith
VISUAL EDITOR:	James Miller, AIFD
ART DIRECTOR:	Ana Maben
FLORAL DESIGN:	Marc Bass, AIFD
	Paula DeClerk
	Perry Walston, AIFD

 Knud Nielsen Company, Inc.

Knud Nielsen Company, in business since 1913, is the world's leading manufacturer and distributor of dried and preserved botanicals.

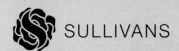 SULLIVANS

Sullivans is a national wholesale distributor offering permanent florals and botanicals, home décor accents, decorative gift items and a complete line of Christmas trimmery.

Florists' Review is the only independent trade magazine for the professional florist in the United States. In addition to serving the needs of retail florists through its monthly publication, the magazine has an active book division that supplies educational products to all who are interested in floral design. For more information, visit *Florists' Review's* Web site at *www.floristsreview.com* or call (800) 367-4708.

Florists' Review's 101 Silk & Dried Designs was designed and produced by Florists' Review Enterprises, Inc., Topeka, Kansas. *www.floristsreview.com*

Printed in the United States by Mainline Printing, Topeka, Kansas.

ISBN:	0-9714860-6-9

contents

spring 4

summer 52

autumn 98

winter 148

Awesome Blossoms

Fabric tulips illustrate some of nature's most gallant handiwork.

Always-impacting parrot tulips, with their trademark bold stripes and ruffly scalloped petals, demonstrate their ability to make a grand statement, even when simply gathered into a radiating hand-tied bouquet.

Here, one dozen of the majestic bulb flowers, accented by *Skimmia* and cascading pepperberries, which echo the foliage's natural tendencies and obscure the mass of stems inside the vase, are dropped into a high-style glass vase. Although the tulips' foliage and stems must be formed into graceful arches, the large glamorous blooms require no shaping.

Use this sumptuous bouquet in spacious entryways and atop large tables and buffets.

1 Flex the tulips' stems and foliage to create a gentle curve, leaving the pristine blossoms untouched.

2 Gather tulips into a bunch in one hand, and add *Skimmia* to the bunch in single-stem insertions.

3 Space pepperberry sprays evenly around the tulip-and-*Skimmia* bouquet. Bind the bouquet with a tie of honeysuckle wire. Drop the bouquet into stemmed vase.

materials:

silk/permanent
parrot tulips
Skimmia
pepperberries
other
honeysuckle wire
stemmed pillar vase

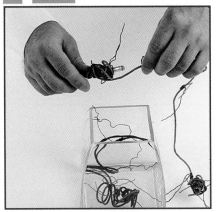

1 Wrap lengths of twig garland around a pencil to form curly tendrils. Tuck the tendrils into the vase.

2 Gather shaped tulips into a bouquet, and tightly bind the stems with waterproof tape.

3 Wrap twig garland around the bundled stems, concealing the waterproof tape. Fan out the stem ends, and bend them slightly to support the bouquet.

Tulip Splendor

Achieve the utmost in realism with purposeful shaping.

A trio of fabric tulip bouquets, each of which includes both buds and blooms in a range of pinks, are separated and reassembled into an amazingly lifelike arrangement that perfectly replicates the peculiar yet natural habits of these exquisite springtime favorites.

Achieving such realism, though, requires shaping of each stem and leaf, so some blossoms, as if reacting to gravity the way their fresh counterparts would, gently cascade over the sides of the vase while others extend upward as if reaching toward the sun.

Inside the chic vessel, the pliable stems are bent slightly at the ends to enable the bouquet to stand upright—the only mechanics required—and swirling tendrils lend movement, color and textural intrigue.

materials:
silk/permanent
tulip bouquets
twig garland
other
waterproof tape
glass vase

Sculpted Callas

Art imitates life with fabric callas shaped inside a clear glass vessel.

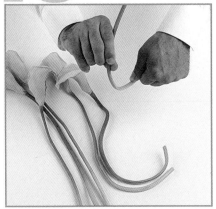

1 Flex the ends of the calla stems to add dynamic curves.

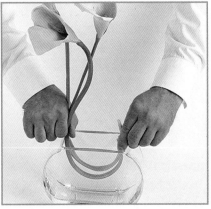

2 Insert one group of callas on one side of the container, and place the other group opposite the first.

3 Tuck the long beaded garland into the vessel, filling the open space.

In both fresh and fabric forms, the long graceful stems of callas can be shaped to create elegant curving lines that, if arranged in clear glass, become important dynamic visual elements—a fact that is masterfully demonstrated in this artful floral sculpture. And, in this context, displayed inside a fish-bowl-shaped oval vessel, the arching stems also serve as the mechanics, keeping the glamorous florals in place.

An effusive garland of green beads, resembling sparkling water, fills the open space between the groups of slender, leafless stems. The beads' bubbly, watery character lends itself to placement of the design in contemporary baths and other modern spaces.

materials:
silk/permanent
  callas
other
  green bead garland
  oval glass vase

Secret Sanctuary

A faux flower bed is home to an avian couple.

1 Fill a moss-covered pot with dry foam. Dip a bird's nest into pan-melt glue, and secure the nest atop the foam.

2 Gently flex the daffodils' stems to add a natural curve. Insert the daffodils into the dry foam on either side of the nest.

3 Hot-glue small tufts of reindeer moss between the nest and the edge of the pot, concealing the dry foam. Clip the birds onto the nest. Hot-glue moss onto the clips to cover them.

Hidden among a vegetative planting of some of spring's first blossoms, a well-constructed bird's nest is home to a pair of expectant gold finches. The diminutive songbirds are simply clipped to the nest and the birds' clips concealed by bits of reindeer moss. Additional tufts of the moss around the nest resemble a grassy ground cover while also concealing the pot's dry foam.

The placement of the radiant daffodils, along with the hand-shaped arching stems, provides a dimensional frame, directing visual attention inward to the avian habitat. Sold in a bouquet composed of both buds and blooms, the florals add botanical realism to the vegetative, as-they-would-grow presentation that is ideal for springtime gift-giving.

materials:

silk/permanent
    daffodil bouquet
dried/preserved
    reindeer moss
    twig nest
other
    gold finches
    dry foam
    pan-melt glue
    hot glue
    mossed pot

Quiet Bouquet

A calming hand-tied collection decorates tranquil spaces.

1 Gather *Gerberas* into a bunch. Arrange remaining materials into a hand-tied bouquet.

2 Bundle the bouquet's stems together using green paddle wire.

3 Cover the wire with a wrapping of ivy vine. Gently flex the ends of the *Gerberas'* stems, so the bouquet will stand upright when dropped into its vase.

The permanent blossoms of pale chartreuse callas and ruffly-petaled pastel pink *Gerberas* combine in a diminutive bouquet to form a complementary color harmony, which, although traditionally vibrant and energetic, is, in its softest form, a soothing springtime palette.

Trailing tendrils of French ivy and cascading cinamomo foliage, which repeats and extends the pastel hues of the *Gerberas*, add dimension to the clustered flowers. Another ivy vine serves as an organic concealment for the wire binding that holds the hand-tied flowers in place. The only other mechanic required is a light manual flexing of the longest stem ends, so the resulting tension will enable the bouquet to stand upright.

materials:
silk/permanent
    callas
    Gerberas
    cinamomo leaves
    miniature French ivy
other
    paddle wire
    glass vase

Vertical Reflections

Graceful lines compose a contemporary two-part arrangement.

At the center of this dynamic vertical design, featuring a pristine *Cymbidium* orchid plant and a cascade of trailing miniature French ivy, a grand pair of *Galax* leaves forms a strong focal area, and the rounded shapes of the leaves, which contrast beautifully with the vertical lines, provides necessary visual weight. The leaf duo also separates the twin elements of the artfully reflective, but not precisely mirrored, composition.

Inside the long-necked, bottle-style vase, several pieces of river cane, glued around the orchid plant's short stem, reinforce the vertical presence and, cut to just the right lengths, act as narrow receptacles for the individual ivy and *Galax* stems.

1 Shape the orchid's leaves and stems for a natural, realistic *Cymbidium* plant presentation.

2 Glue several pieces of river cane around the stem of the orchid plant, leaving the trailing roots exposed.

3 Insert the stems of the *Galax* leaves and ivy into the hollow river cane. Secure in place with glue if desired.

materials:

silk/permanent
Cymbidium orchid plant
mini French ivy
Galax leaves
dried/preserved
river cane
other
pan-melt glue
bottle vase

Springtime Snowballs

Flower-filled branches make a spectacular spring display.

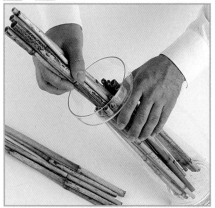

1 Cut river cane into lengths that will extend just into the candleholder/vase basin. Drop the river cane, thicker ends first, into the container.

2 Clip *Viburnum* stems to varying lengths to achieve a somewhat vertical column, and insert the flowers' stems into the hollow river cane.

3 Arrange berries around the container's rim to form a collar.

Inside a tall glass candleholder/vase, several branches of *Viburnums*, laden with the showy springtime blossoms, are arranged into a resplendent column that showcases the dazzling snowball-like inflorescences.

Like most vertical line-mass compositions, a focal point at the container's rim, provided here by green cranberries whose lavish fruit-filled sprays tumble over the sides of the vessel, adds much-needed balance to the statuesque structure. A tight massing of river cane serves as the mechanics and disguises the short stem ends of the berry picks.

The design, with its soothing neutral palette and feminine appeal, would be stunning on a lady's vanity or a glass coffee table.

materials:
silk/permanent
   Viburnums
   green cranberry picks
dried/preserved
   river cane
other
   glass candleholder/vase

Permanent Drop-In

Fabric *Ranunculi* and painted drieds effectively fill a standard cylinder.

Arrangements in glass are as tricky for permanent designs as they are for fresh. With the absence of dry foam, it's always a challenge to make a modest number of stems fill a receptacle and stand securely in place.

However, an inventive maze of wildly swirling panchu springs can easily accomplish that goal. The lively curves and twists establish a grid, or armature, so just a few stems of lifelike fabric *Ranunculi* and a trio of green bell cups are able to stand upright and compose a pleasing mass.

A simple tie of wired ribbon adds an appropriate accent as well as a balance of descending lines in reverse proportion to the main composition.

materials:
dried/preserved
  party panchu springs
  party bell cups
silk/permanent
  Ranunculi
other
  green aluminum wire
  wired ribbon
  cylinder vase

1 Enwrap glass cylinder with wired ribbon, and tie a decorative knot. Shape the wired streamers for a flowing dynamic.

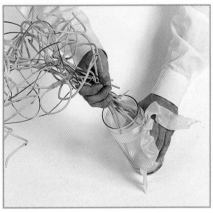

2 Gather panchu springs and curled aluminum wire into a loose bundle, and drop them into a cylinder vase.

3 Position flowers and bell cups into the panchu-spring-and-wire armature.

Landscaped Garden

Groups of fabric flowers portray a cultivated planting.

1 Fill a pedestal bowl with dry foam, and top the foam with moss. Place *Irises* into foam in a group on one end of the bowl, varying the heights for a natural, garden-grown appearance.

2 Add a few branches of flowering almond between the *Irises* and the bowl's rim. Place another group of flowering almond into the foam at the end of the bowl opposite the *Irises*.

3 Arrange remaining materials in consecutively lower groupings. At the design's base, insert berries and ferns to flow over the rim. Finish with velvet pansies spaced evenly around the base.

With its weathered patina, this lichen-covered urn appears to have been salvaged from among the ruins of a long-forgotten garden but now finds new life displaying a vibrant palette of spring's bounty.

Inside the oval bowl, a carefully cultivated garden landscape is elegantly rendered with an abundant "planting" of spring-blooming beauties. The *Irises*, true to the botanical format, are presented in developmental stages that range from bud to full bloom. And at the base, densely placed materials represent a lush ground cover.

Utilize this grand landscaped composition in traditional settings with ample space to allow it to shine brilliantly.

materials:
silk/permanent
Irises
snapdragons
flowering almond
velvet pansies
Gomphrena globes
green cranberries
Coleus
fern fronds
dried/preserved
crown flowers
mood moss
other
dry foam
lichen-covered oval urn

Songs of Spring

A forgotten spring garden is depicted through vegetative design.

1 Detach the bird from its stake, and glue the stake into the center of a dry foam-filled urn. Drop the angel vine kissing balls onto the stake.

2 Replace the resin bird atop its stake.

3 Glue velvet pansies and a few forget-me-nots around the container's perimeter. Glue additional forget-me-nots into the stack of vine-covered balls.

Perched atop what resembles an untended shrub that's become entangled by vining blossoms, a carefree songbird chortles the melodious praises of a renewed spring season. The cheery wren is sold attached to a metal stake, which is glued into dry foam inside a lichen-covered urn. The container's weathered finish enhances the design's nature-made realism.

Angel vine kissing balls, threaded onto the bird's stake, compose the vertical shrub on which pale blue forget-me-nots, tucked into the vine ball stack, are entwined. And short-stemmed deep-purple pansies, which sprout from around the shrub's base, balance its overall height.

materials:
silk/permanent
  velvet pansies
  forget-me-nots
dried/preserved
  angel vine kissing balls
  reindeer moss
other
  dry foam
  pan-melt glue
  bird on a stake
  lichen urn

Spring Bounty

Embrace the lush blooming beginning of each new year.

1 Glue *Petunias* into a ready-made smilax wreath. Add remaining materials in bounteous layers, starting with those of the darkest hues.

2 Dip the butterflies' wire stems into pan-melt glue, and adhere the wires into the wreath.

3 Tie a bow out of 4-inch ribbon, and dip a small portion of the bow's backside into pan-melt glue. Attach the bow into the center of the lower half of the wreath.

Typically fall, the harvest season, is considered the season of plenty, but spring, with new crops of perennials springing up and fresh annuals ready for planting, has its bounty, too.

Constructed atop a ready-made smilax wreath form, with textural layers of ravishing petunias, *Scabiosa* pods, green cranberries and striking bicolor *Coleus* leaves, spring's abundance is beautifully demonstrated in this lush wreath. With the addition of a trio of migrating monarch butterflies returning home for the season, an energetic triadic color harmony is achieved.

This bountiful wreath is gorgeous for display on doors as well as on walls in kitchens, garden rooms and other sunwashed spaces.

materials:
silk/permanent
> Petunias
> Coleuses
> *Scabiosa* pods
> green cranberries
> smilax wreath

other
> wide silk ribbon
> pan-melt glue

Dayglow Panchu

Painted drieds and faux garden blossoms combine for a bold greeting.

Energetic swirls of electric purple and hot pink panchu springs are wired together to form the base of a dynamic, phosphorescent wreath that is sure to invigorate winter-weary exteriors. Even a covered porch will be brightened by its effulgent presence, much of which emanates from bold bell cups in coordinating pink and purple hues as well as from vivid orbs formed of sisal and bound with decorative wire.

The addition of fabric *Zinnias*, sporting coordinating pink-striped petals, faux *Gomphrena* globes and texture-rich variegated *Coleus* complete this jocund seasonal accessory, which is vibrant, youthful, and totally engaging to view.

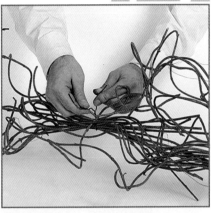

1 Assemble a garland of pink and purple panchu springs by haphazardly wiring them together. Form the panchu garland into a wreath, and secure the ends together with more wire.

2 Compact several masses of sisal into balls, and wrap each sisal orb with silver wire. Attach sisal orbs and bell cups to the panchu base with additional wire or glue.

3 Glue flowers and foliage onto the wreath, and finish the wreath by adding a few decorative swirls of silver wire.

materials:

dried/preserved
party panchu springs
party bell cups
pink sisal

silk/permanent
miniature *Dahlias*
Coleus sprays
Gomphrena globes

other
silver wire
purple wire
pink wire
pan-melt glue

Spring Greetings

A radiant wreath welcomes guests.

Golden preserved roses, elegant green *Hydrangeas* and intriguing green yarrow lavishly decorate a fern-enhanced base that is enlarged by the addition of honeysuckle vine secured into the wreath's center. The added vine widens the wreath base and enables a larger "canvas" onto which the luxuriant materials can be artfully arranged.

The oversized composition, which is rich with the textures of feathery fern fronds and a berried garland woven among the blossoms, can bedeck a wall or door, or even be laid atop a table, beginning in spring and continuing throughout the summer.

1 Swirl Asian honeysuckle vine around the interior of a smilax wreath, weaving some of the vine's tendrils into the wreath base to hold the vine in place.

2 Dip the stem ends of fan fern into pan-melt glue, and insert the fronds around the perimeter of the wreath base. Arrange *Hydrangeas*, roses and yarrow into the wreath and vines.

3 Attach wood picks to each end of a berry garland. Dip one pick into pan-melt glue, and secure it to the wreath form. Weave the garland among the blossoms, and secure the other end into the base.

materials:

dried/preserved
  roses
  Hydrangeas
  yarrow
  fan fern
  Asian honeysuckle vine
  smilax wreath
silk/permanent
  berry garland
other
  wood picks
  pan-melt glue

Door Sheath

A basketful of garden bounty is transformed into door and wall décor.

1 Assemble bells-of-Ireland and open roses into a sheaf. Bind with waterproof tape. Bend rose stems to position blossoms.

2 Assemble lavender into a bundle, and bind with tape or an organic-looking binding such as twig garland. Glue the lavender bundle atop the bundle of stems.

3 Add cilantro garnish, and weave berried garland into the grouping. Insert a wood pick into the amaryllis bulb, and glue it onto the door sheath.

Resembling a freshly picked springtime harvest that has been laid into a gathering basket, downward-pointing bells-of-Ireland, whose stems mingle with thorn-covered rose stems, form a captivating vertical line. At its center, a dramatic focal area is created with enchanting open roses, a bunch of dried lavender, cilantro and a budding amaryllis bulb with roots still intact, all of which is surrounded by a garland of pepperberries that fills out the oval form and adds important contrasting colors and textures.

The result is a slim, inverted-looking sheath with a strong vertical presence, so it's ideal for hanging on narrow interior doors and walls in small spaces.

materials:
silk/permanent
 amaryllis bulb
 open roses
 bells-of-Ireland
 pepperberry garland
 cilantro
dried/preserved
 lavender
other
 waterproof tape
 pan-melt glue
 wood pick

Decorative Tableware

Showcase collections and enhance home décor.

Vintage tableware items are popular collectibles, and, when combined with a well-treated plate holder like this one, they make an idyllic display, especially in convivial spaces such as kitchen and dining areas.

In this magnificent example, exotic-looking passion flower vine is entwined around the frame of a wrought iron plate holder that features twiglike accents upon which a warbling songbird is perched.

Accessorize the arboreous plate holders for those who have their own collections, or drop by antiques stores for affordable mismatched pieces to create your own complete offerings. And easily adapt the concept with different ribbon and other vining blossoms.

1 Starting at the tip of the plate holder, entwine passion flower vine around one side of the holder's wrought iron frame. Allow the vine to cascade beyond the bottom of the frame.

2 Form pistachio ribbon into a bow with chevron ends. Tie on an additional length of ribbon as a tail.

3 Tie the bow onto the wrought iron frame with additional lengths of ribbon.

materials:
silk/permanent
 passion flower vine
other
 wire-edged ribbon
 bird plate holder

Flight of Fancy

Traditional design is paired with an innovative, sprightly container.

A winged cherub, elevated atop a narrow stake, and its companion urn are two parts of a single novel design accessory that, with its weathered patina, is ideal for a traditional garden nosegay of spray roses and snapdragons in a charming complementary color harmony.

Willow branches, foliated with wispy green leaves, are gathered around the stake and secured with a tie of organic-looking twig garland to beautifully frame the angelic figure and contribute to the design's fancifully implied animation.

The winsome composition, a classical expression for spring, will gloriously enhance any feminine space.

1 Remove the cherub from its stake. Impale a block of dry foam with the stake, and push the foam into the urn. Replace cherub onto stake.

2 Insert willow branches into foam, and gather branches around the stake. Tie twig garland around branches, to secure them to the stake. Curl the ends of the twig vine around a pencil.

3 Place spray roses and snapdragons into the foam-filled urn in nosegay arrangement. Fill voids with rose leaves.

materials:

silk/permanent
spray roses with leaves
snapdragons
willow branches
twig garland

other
dry foam
pan-melt glue
flying cherub container

Cottontail Whimsy

A charming accessory helps to capture the essence of spring.

Perched atop its baluster, a white bunny is caught in the act of frolicking in a blooming springtime garden in this resplendent arrangement that imparts the innocence and gaiety often associated with the season of rebirth and renewal.

For the utmost in organic realism, the mesmeric floral mix—fabric, dried and preserved materials used together—is arranged into a mossy pot, and bunches of dried lavender, inserted in what appears to be a haphazard manner, bestows an uncultivated character.

Pleasingly feminine and cheery, this serene garden is divine on display in garden rooms, kitchens and other sunny spaces.

1 Glue reindeer moss around the point where the bunny and baluster meet. Fill a moss-covered pot with dry foam. Dip the baluster base into pan-melt glue, and adhere atop the foam.

2 Conceal the exposed foam with reindeer moss, and arrange *Galax* leaves around the pot in a collar formation.

3 Assemble lavender into bundles. Secure by twisting short bits of honeysuckle wire around the bundles. Wire a wood pick to the honeysuckle wire twists, and insert the pick into foam.

materials:

silk/permanent
    garden *Ranunculi*
    velvet pansies
    thyme
    Galax leaves
dried/preserved
    Hydrangeas
    lavender
    reindeer moss
other
    bunny on baluster
    wired wood picks
    dry foam
    pan-melt glue
    honeysuckle wire
    mossed pot

Gardenia Topiary

Create an enchanting accent in just a few simple steps.

1 Fill a moss-covered pot with dry foam. Entwine a pair of *Gardenia* stems to form a topiary. Insert the topiary into the foam.

2 Hot-glue bits of reindeer moss atop the dry foam. Glue the base of a small nest, and secure the nest into the mossed foam with florist wire bent into a "hairpin."

3 Glue additional moss around the bird's nest. Clip birds onto the nest and *Gardenia* stems. Conceal the clips with moss.

Despite its ordered assembly and tailored detailing, this gracious bird-enhanced topiary is quick and easy to construct and requires just a few basic materials, starting with two stems of *Gardenias*, on which the blooms and foliages are clustered at the stems' tips.

The flowers' lengthy, bare stems are casually interwoven, forming a modest massing of blossoms and foliage atop a slightly entangled tree "trunk." The tree is simply inserted into a diminutive mossed pot filled with dry foam and accessorized with charming chickadees, a nest and mossy coverings.

The tiny topiary makes a great springtime gift and can send cherry get-well greetings.

materials:
silk/permanent
  Gardenias
dried/preserved
  miniature twig and grass nest
  reindeer moss
other
  chickadees with clips
  florist wire
  dry foam
  hot glue
  mossed pot

Absolute Showstopper

Realistic plants and sprays resemble an exquisite potted orchid.

1 Fill an urn with dry foam, and disguise the foam with mood moss. Insert orchid plants into the foam, leaving the faux roots exposed to resemble orchids' natural growth habits.

2 Insert orchid sprays into the foam near the orchid plant foliage, so plants appear to have multiple orchid sprays.

3 Accessorize design with badam nuts and *Skimmia*. Insert seeded birch branches to fill the void between the orchid sprays.

Two *Phalaenopsis* orchid plants, complete with foliage and roots, and two orchid sprays, all of which are filled with the crimson mothlike blooms and plump, ready-to-open buds, comprise this majestic, true-to-life composition. The plants' roots, in true vegetative form, overflow from within the container, as their fresh, planted counterparts would.

Among the bare roots and foliage, which are accented by badam nut pods, pale green *Skimmias* lighten the dark palette at the base. Repeating the soft greens imparted by the tufted blossoms, and filling the negative space between the pair of tall arching sprays, are lofty catkin-laden birch branches, which reinforce the complementary color palette.

materials:
silk/permanent
  Phalaenopsis orchid plants with leaves
  Phalaenopsis orchid
  Skimmia
  birch sprays
dried/preserved
  badam nut pods
  mood moss
other
  dry foam
  urn

Nesting Instincts

Embrace spring through nature's unspoiled beauty.

1 Form two bunches of wild grass into nest-like swirls. Attach the grassy bunch to the dry foam inside the basket with six or eight hairpin wires.

2 Dip the ends of several birch branches into pan-melt glue, and tuck the glued ends into the grassy swirls.

3 Tuck loose bits of angel vines, fern, mosses and other materials into the center of the grasses, for a realistic nest effect. Add wooden eggs.

The idyllic qualities of spring, a season equated with renewal and rebirth, are no more clearly expressed than in this organic nest creation, which is filled with a trio of newly laid eggs.

Creating the avian abode starts with a rustic woven basket, into which the nestlike structure is built. Dry foam inside the basket, which fills the container to about 1 inch below its rim, supports two bunches of wild grass that are fashioned into an untamed swirl and pinned to the foam. Loose bits of angel vine, fern, mosses and other organic materials are amassed inside the grass while birch branches are glued into the grassy perimeter, for a realistic nest presentation.

materials:

dried/preserved
  wild grass
  birch twigs
  fan fern
  moss
  angel vine
other
  wooden eggs
  woven basket
  hairpin wires
  pan-melt glue

Three Rings

Wreath-wrapped florals show Biedermeier influence.

1 Form honeysuckle garland and leafy vine into a wreath. Secure with honeysuckle wire. Using leftover wire bent into "hairpins," attach the wreath atop a cylindrical pot filled with a column of dry foam that extends 1 inch above the pot's rim.

2 Arrange cone flowers in a ring around the inside of the wreath form. Fill the wreath's opening with moss.

3 Clip yarrow stems, so they're all the same length. Starting at the outer edge and working inward, fill the wreath center with yarrow. Pack yarrow tightly to form a small mound.

The concentric rings typical of Biedermeier design take an atypical organic twist in this elevated structure that, with its leafy enhancements, is less orderly than the traditional circular composition.

At the design's center, a ring of cone flowers surrounds a rounded mass of yarrow, both of whose intense burgundy hues complement the diminutive foliage, which is wired to a custom-assembled wreath form made from Asian honeysuckle garland.

Given its untamed appearance, this elevated structure would best beautify informal settings and could remain in place year-round, even during the holiday season.

materials:
dried/preserved
  yarrow
  cone flowers
  Asian honeysuckle garland
  reindeer moss
silk/permanent
  leaf garland
other
  dry foam
  honeysuckle wire
  hairpin wires
  cylindrical pot

22

Energetic Profusion

A lush mounded design erupts with color and texture.

1 Dip pomegranates in pan-melt glue, attach to birch branches, and secure with wire. Cover the glue and wire with tufts of reindeer moss.

2 Gather reserved barley stems into sheaflike bundles. Wrap the bundles with waterproof tape, and secure a short dowel or saved stick to the center of each bundle for insertion into dry foam.

3 Arrange the birch branches into the foam. Add the barley bundles in X-like pairs, and cover the binding points with *Hydrangeas* and other blossoms. Finish the arrangement in rounded formation.

Wonderful atop almost any large table, this glorious mound of colorful blossoms and barley bundles can invigorate a variety of home and office environments.

For the most exciting bursts of color, the brilliantly hued daisies, as well as some pomegranates attached to birch branches, are grouped together, and the open spaces are then filled with *Hydrangea* blossoms and salal leaves. (It's best to insert *Hydrangeas* and any other somewhat delicate materials last, to avoid damage.)

Since the botanicals are used in abundance, and the pomegranate-embellished branches cascade over the container's sides, a heavy or weighted container is required.

materials:

dried/preserved
Hydrangeas
sand daisies
pomegranates
birch branches
salal leaves
reindeer moss
barley stems

other
short dowels or reserved sticks
thin-gauge wire
waterproof tape
dry foam
pan-melt glue
heavy or weighted container

23

Wooded Frame

Untamed branches shroud a rose and berry planting.

With an organically inspired tortoiseshell finish, this footed metal planter is an ideal receptacle for a botanical gathering featuring luminous preserved yellow roses and delicate pink pepperberries. Tufts of mood moss, in a vibrant color-enhanced hue, are tucked in among the blossoms, and the pepperberries, wired into clusters for easy insertion, are arranged into the mossy tufts. For dimension and texture, several barely budding faux branches are placed around the planter's perimeter, creating a rambling frame that directs attention to the ordered composition within.

The design's size, along with its contrasting textures, makes it well-suited for placement throughout the home.

1 Fill a metal planter with dry foam that extends 4 inches above the rim. Arrange roses. Using hairpin wires, secure tufts of mood moss into the foam around the roses.

2 Hot-glue wired clusters of pepperberries in and among the rose blossoms.

3 Insert faux vines around the perimeter of the arrangement. Gently bend the pliable branches into an arching framework.

materials:
dried/preserved
  roses
  pepperberries
  mood moss
  birch branches
other
  plastic foam
  hot glue
  hairpin wires
  footed metal planter

Bundled Herbs

Lavender bundles top a mounded array of gardeny materials.

Inside an elegant metal basin that is enhanced with a charming floral motif, a luxurious collection of roses, sweet Williams, pepperberries and pomegranates is arranged into a gorgeous mass of garden-gathered botanicals that appear to overflow from within the pretty container. Bundles of lavender, wired to wood picks for secure placement, are positioned atop the florid mound in balanced placements, adding textural interest and additional color to the mostly monochromatic design.

This feminine selection is wonderful for spring but offers consumers additional value since it can remain in homes, especially traditional settings, throughout the year.

1 Pierce the base of each pomegranate to make a hole. Using hot glue, secure a leftover stem or wood pick into each hole.

2 Arrange sweet Williams and other materials into dry foam that extends 6 inches above the container's rim. Bundle lavender, and secure the bundles with wired wood picks.

3 Fill open spaces with rose leaves, adhered with just a small dab of hot glue.

materials:
dried/preserved
  roses
  pomegranates
  pepperberries
  sweet Williams
  lavender
silk/permanent
  rose foliage
other
  hot glue
  leftover stems or wood picks
  tin container

Classical Dome

Summery filler flower takes center stage.

Lavish bunches of yarrow, in a luscious persimmon hue, are arranged into a foam sphere to create this exquisite textural mound, which could accessorize many types of home and office settings.

To achieve the uniform rounded silhouette, the yarrow's stems are all trimmed to the same length, and the blossoms are placed into the foam sphere in a dense cluster. At the base of the yarrow, small clumps of reindeer moss conceal the foam, and delicate tendrils of angel vine are tightly wrapped to form a wispy collar.

With its warm palette and traditional stylings, this consummate piece, which will sell well in pairs, can be displayed throughout the summer and fall.

1 Clip yarrow stems to about 2 inches in length. Insert the stems into a plastic-foam sphere.

2 Tuck small clumps of reindeer moss beneath the yarrow mass to fill any gaps and conceal the foam.

3 Wrap tendrils of angel vine tightly around the arrangement's base. Secure with hairpin-shaped wires.

materials:
dried/preserved
  yarrow
  reindeer moss
  angel vine
other
  hairpin wires
  plastic-foam sphere
  urn

Berried Treasure

Cherished blossoms dazzle amid contrasting colors and a vintage vessel.

A French-inspired urn, with delicate scrolled handles, is manufactured with an aged patina for an antique look that makes it the perfect vessel for displaying a lavish mound of exquisite *Hydrangeas*, an old-fashioned garden favorite. Set against a collar of laurel leaves and berry sprays in the deepest purple hues, the ruffly pale green florets, some of which are lightly tinged with a russet edge, shine all the more brilliantly.

While these remarkably lifelike flowers closely replicate fresh-cut *Hydrangeas*, they offer one benefit over their thirsty counter-parts: they are guaranteed wilt-free!

Place this gorgeous selection, which easily scales up or down, practically anywhere in the home, and display throughout summer.

1 Clip a laurel leaf and berries plant into small sections, each containing just a few leaves. Insert the clipped branchlets into foam at an angle to form a leafy collar.

2 Insert berry sprays into the leafy collar, placing berries around the pot's perimeter.

3 Place *Hydrangeas* into foam, inside the berry and leaf collar, in a mounded formation.

materials:
silk/permanent
 Hydrangeas
 berries
 laurel and berries plant
other
 foam
 urn

Good Libations

Bordeaux-colored blossoms overflow a goblet-style container.

Inside what resembles a super-sized cocktail glass, slender blades of dune grass are spun to form a textural bed inside which a small block of foam is concealed. The grasses' natural coloring strikes a soothing balance for the frothy collection of intensely hued *Hydrangeas* that are arranged into the foam.

For a more tightly clustered *Hydrangea* mound, bind the tiny branchlets of the inflorescence, just beneath the florets, with stem wrap. The clustered blossoms will also support the *Anemones*, which are inserted through the *Hydrangeas* and into the foam.

Easily adapted to a variety of seasons, this florid goblet is great for parties, so suggest that customers purchase them in multiples.

1 Swirl a lavish bundle of dune grass around the inside of the container.

2 Nestle a small block of foam into the center of the dune grass swirls.

3 Arrange *Hydrangeas* into a mound. Insert *Anemone* stems through the *Hydrangea* florets in random placements.

materials:
silk/permanent
   Anemones
dried/preserved
   Hydrangeas
   dune grass
other
   candleholder/bowl

Trio of Tones

Fuchsia *Hydrangeas* trim light pink roses inside a medium pink pot.

1 Insert *Hydrangea* blossoms into dry foam to form a collar around the pot's circumference.

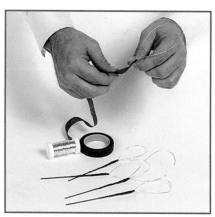

2 Attach lengths of heavy-gauge wire to each rose blossom. Encircle each rose with a *Magnolia* leaf, and secure the leaves with stem wrap. Place the roses into the foam in a mounded formation.

3 Create loops of aluminum wire, and wrap the loose ends with stem wrap to create a "stem" for insertion into the foam. Arrange the wire loops amid the leaf-wrapped roses.

Reminiscent of a mounded European tussie-mussie, this adorable pink-on-pink composition makes a delightful gift, especially for a hostess at a carefree summer gathering.

The pretty design is composed of perennially feminine pastel-pink roses that are formed into a dome inside a deeper-pink pot. Separating the two similar tones is a chic band of hot-pink *Hydrangeas* that trims the rosy mound. Adding to the drama, fabric *Magnolia* leaves, which enwrap the delicate roses, achieve a vibrant complementary color harmony with the trio of pink tones.

This glorious gathering is accessorized with sparkling loops of aluminum wire and will display beautifully in multiples.

materials:
dried/preserved
 roses
 Hydrangeas
silk/permanent
 Magnolia leaves
other
 aluminum wire
 heavy-gauge wire
 dry foam
 ceramic container

Ring Around the Roses

Preserved pink roses are hidden within a hedge of lavender.

Two bunches of dried lavender, banded onto a tall clay pot, form an intriguing herb perimeter into which a bouquet of preserved but very-fresh-looking roses is arranged in a pavé manner. The tightly packed, level bloom placements, typical of the pavé style, make the roses appear to be cloaked inside the well-groomed boundaries of a secret lavender garden.

This carefully structured accessory, which is tailored with a preserved band of salal leaves and a smart bow-tie of pretty ribbon, balances ordered formality with enough grace and femininity to befit girls' rooms, bathrooms, and other intimate spaces.

1 Place a rubber band onto a tall clay pot, and insert bunches of lavender beneath the band, so the band holds the herbs in place. Continue inserting bunches until the pot is surrounded.

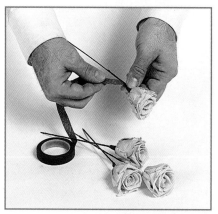

2 Add stems to preserved roses by piercing each bloom with heavy-gauge wire and securing the wire to the rose with a wrapping of floral tape. Arrange roses inside the lavender perimeter.

3 Hot-glue large salal leaves onto the pot's exterior in overlapping layers to conceal the banding on the lavender. Finish with a tie of coordinating ribbon.

materials:
dried/preserved
  roses
  lavender
  salal leaves
  Spanish moss
other
  ribbon
  heavy-gauge wire
  floral tape
  rubber bands
  hot glue
  dry foam
  tall clay pot

Blue Basket

A garden hedge blossoms amid a frame of vine-covered branches.

1 Bundle short clusters of clipped birch branches, and attach the bundles to wood picks with barked wire. Place the birch bundles around the perimeter of a foam-filled twig basket.

Reflecting the shape of its woodsy twig container, a rectangular burst of statice is pavéd inside natural blue lavender that outlines a foam block into which the materials are arranged. Round globe-thistle detailing surrounds the rectangular structure with an appealing contrast of shapes.

The result is an orderly hedge of blue blossoms that appears to have erupted amid an untended woodlands, represented by birch twigs entwined by permanent smilax vine. The vine-covered branches frame the manicured floral thicket and direct attention to the geometric forms it comprises.

This striking basket, despite its summery appeal, can beautify a home year-round.

2 Insert branches into the foam to make a "handle." Attach horizontal branches with barked wire. Wind foliage vine around the handle, and collar the foam with boxwood.

materials:
dried/preserved
   statice
   lavender
   globe thistle
   boxwood
   birch branches
silk/permanent
   smilax vine
other
   barked wire
   dry foam
   twig basket

3 Place lavender into the foam's perimeter, leaving the center vacant. Fill the center with statice. Grasping the globe thistles at their stems, insert them around the lavender in collar formation.

Wreath-Topped Bowl

A traditional decorative receives an unexpected treatment.

1 Trim the rose stems to about 2 inches in length. Dip the clipped stems into pan-melt glue, and position them onto a *Eucalyptus* wreath. Glue *Hydrangeas* and cranberries onto the wreath.

2 Trim the pineapples' stems to about 2 inches in length. Dip them into pan-melt glue, and place them into the wreath at an angle.

3 Place the completed wreath atop the pedestal bowl.

Preserved snowflake *Hydrangeas* and a wealth of fabric flowers generously spill over the sides of a serene pedestal bowl, which elevates the ready-made *Eucalyptus* wreath base into which the materials are lavishly arranged. While this luxurious centerpiece may be laid atop a table, or even hung on a wall, placement on a pedestaled vessel heightens its impact and invites viewers to examine its dimensions and depth.

The materials, in a family of soothing monochromatic greens, include captivating faux pineapples—symbols of hospitality. These welcoming fruits are delightful additions to this composition, which can decorate a variety of tables in traditional spaces.

materials:
dried/preserved
  snowflake *Hydrangeas*
silk/permanent
  velvet roses
  pineapples
  green cranberry picks
  Eucalyptus wreath
other
  pan-melt glue
  bowl on pedestal

1 Place dry foam inside the container. Form barley into bunches, and attach a steel pick to each. Insert the picked bunches into the foam to create a row. Repeat barley insertions in the opposite end of the foam.

2 Continue inserting floral materials into the foam in ordered rows, working inward from the outside edges of the container.

3 Dip reindeer moss into pan-melt glue, and tuck it around the container's edges to conceal exposed foam.

Mirror Image

Floral materials are grouped into artfully reflective rows.

Distinctly defined groups of materials, which include a textural sensation of natural barley and color-enhanced *Proteas* and chico chokes, are arranged into precise rows, resulting in a dramatic striped appearance.

But perhaps what's most intriguing about this creative striped composition is that, through a design technique known as "mirroring," each half of the symmetrical design is a reflection of the other. The ordered rows, along with the visual stimulation of mirroring, achieve an artistically polished feel.

The design's formality, as well as its rich textures and complementary color palette, allow it to remain on display from summer through fall.

materials:
dried/preserved
  barley
  Proteas
  chico chokes
  reindeer moss
other
  steel picks
  dry foam
  rectangular container

Found Nest

1. Affix a plastic-foam sphere atop a clay pot with hot glue. Hot-glue two wood picks into a bird's nest, and insert the picks into the foam sphere.

2. Lay bundles of lavender onto the foam in random placements, covering the sphere. Secure each bundle into the foam with Dixon pins. Fill in open areas with other materials.

3. Pull the cluster of angel vine apart, and lay it atop the arrangement in a veiling manner, tucking portions of it around other botanicals to hold it in place.

An organic massing conceals an egg-filled habitat.

Hidden amid what resembles an overgrown field of flowers and other botanicals, including sand daisies, yarrow, poppy pods and bundles of lavender all shrouded by a veiling of angel vine, a well-camouflaged bird's nest appears to have been built in place by the very robin responsible for the trio of blue eggs inside. Clipped bits of ostrich feathers line the nest and add to its avian realism.

To maintain the consistent round form while using such a wealth of shapely materials, the bundles of lavender are lavishly laid onto the foam in random placements, with some of the stem ends pointing upward and some pointing down. The remaining materials fill out the shape of the botanical orb.

materials:
dried/preserved
  sand daisies
  lavender
  yarrow
  poppy pods
  bracken fern
  angel vine
  reindeer moss
  bird's nest
other
  ostrich feathers
  Dixon pins
  hot glue
  plastic-foam sphere
  clay pot

Organic Wreath

Sunflowers rest peacefully among untamed fruited branches.

1 Assemble apple branches into a garland, securing them together with honeysuckle wire. Then, swirl the branchy garland into a wreath form.

2 Weave sunflower stems into the wreath structure.

3 Lay the wreath atop a large bowl or platter.

Faux branches laden with apples, as if gathered from an indigenous grove, are bound into fruited garlands and graciously swirled into a natural wreath possessing a simple, uncontrived beauty that reflects the serenity and quietude of lazy summer evenings.

In addition to its organic allure, the branchy wreath functions as an armature for a trio of resplendent golden sunflowers along with petal-free sunflower buds. The florals' stems are simply woven among the boughs and the resulting composition laid atop a vintage-inspired platter.

The wreath's lush low profile recommends it for tabletop placement, especially dining tables and coffee tables.

materials:
silk/permanent
apple branches
sunflowers
other
honeysuckle wire
platter

1 Gather day lilies into a bundle, positioning blooms to create a spherical formation. Just beneath the sphere, bind the stems with honeysuckle wire. Trim stem ends to a uniform length.

2 Fill the urn with foam, and glue mood moss atop the foam to disguise it. Insert bundled lilies into the center of the foam-filled urn.

3 Encircle lily stems with *Hypericum* berries and mint in a hedgelike cluster. Insert thyme around the container's perimeter, weaving the stems together for a tangled appearance.

Lily Topiary

A celestial-inspired orb towers above a planting of berries and herbs.

Luminous day lilies, aglow with sunsplashed radiance, compose a majestic topiary for summer-through-fall display in grand entryways and upon hearths and mantels in both home and office environments.

The ravishing gold and orange blossoms are simply bundled into a petalous sphere atop their statuesque, foliage-free stems. *Hypericum*, into which sprigs of mint plants are interspersed, is placed as if growing around the topiary's base like an unclipped fruited shrub, which is collared by a groundcoverlike display of tangly thyme.

With its weighty iron look, the aged urn is an ideal foil to visually balance the lily orb's immense proportions.

materials:
silk/permanent
  day lilies
  Hypericum berries
  mint plant
  thyme
dried/preserved
  mood moss
other
  dry foam
  pan-melt glue
  honeysuckle wire
  urn

Rose-Topped Cone

Exotic reeds showcase a radiant sphere of perfectly preserved roses.

1 Cut Nile reed in half, and assemble the reed into a bundle. Bind the reed bundle at the bottom with barked wire, and twist the ends to form a shock. Glue the shock into the foam-filled pot.

2 Place mood moss onto a foam sphere, and wrap it with wire to secure in place. Continue until the lower half of the sphere is covered with moss.

3 Insert a hyacinth stake into the foam sphere. Nestle the sphere into the center of the Nile reed bundle, and insert the hyacinth stake into the foam-filled pot. Arrange roses into plastic foam.

For contemporary interiors, this majestic architectural display, with a modern aesthetic, makes a statement on its own but would be even more impacting in multiples that are repeated in the home or office.

Strong vertical lines created by long Nile reeds, with subtle movement expressed through a slight twist of the bundle, contribute to the drama and direct attention upward to the rose-covered sphere. The preserved blooms, which closely resemble fresh, are wired for insertion into the foam.

Nestled amid the Nile reed bundle, the rosy orb, into which a hyacinth stake is inserted, is secured into the foam-filled pot for a secure, long-lasting presentation.

materials:
dried/preserved
  roses
  Nile reed
  mood moss
other
  barked wire
  thin-gauge wire
  hyacinth stake
  plastic-foam sphere
  cylindrical pot

Berried Shrub

A petite bush comprises berries and leaves in a monochromatic palette.

1 Arrange a bundle of birch branches in a fan pattern inside a foam-filled vessel. Trim the branches to a uniform height. Conceal the foam with vertically inserted salal leaves.

2 Cut a plastic foam sphere in half. Dip the flat side of one of the halves into pan-melt glue, and press the half sphere onto the trimmed birch branches.

3 Gather salal leaves into groups, and insert the leafy groups into the foam until the sphere is covered. Clip the berry sprays into two smaller groupings, and arrange them among the leaves.

In a foam-filled metal pot that sits inside a French wire basket, a diminutive shrub is assembled of birch branches, salal leaves and permanent green berries.

The salal, which is placed into the foam sphere in small bunches, is also used as an unexpected material to conceal mechanics, rather than the traditional moss.

With its soothing monochromatic color harmony and overall color uniformity, this pleasing design will coordinate with many interior styles and can be easily adapted to enhance a variety of interior color palettes. The fruited bush could also be sold in multiples and arranged in composite form like a decorative thicket atop a summer party table.

materials:
dried/preserved
 salal
 birch branches
silk/permanent
 green berries
other
 dry foam
 plastic-foam sphere
 pan-melt glue
 pot in wire basket

Herb Topiary

Inverted faux greenery composes a geometric "planting."

Gathered permanent herbs, secured in lavish overlapping layers to a river cane "tree trunk," appear to be hung upside-down for drying while forming a striking textural tree that is topped, in creative finial fashion, with a vine-covered kissing ball.

The unsculpted form, which is assembled starting at the base, is displayed in a classic Roman vase filled with foam. Reindeer moss and lichens cover the mechanics and coordinate with the container's weathered finish. And concealing the final layer of stem ends—those of the slender chives—a band of mood moss is glued beneath the vined orb.

1 To form the lowest layer of greenery, encircle the river cane with willow branches, and secure with honeysuckle wire.

2 Position herbs, starting with mint, in downward-pointing layers, spaced so that, when hanging, each slightly overlaps the previous layer. Secure each layer with honeysuckle wire.

3 With a chenille stem, paint glue onto topmost stems. Thread kissing ball onto glued stems; glue mood moss around ball's base. Insert topiary into foam-filled Roman vase. Apply moss and lichens.

materials:

silk/permanent
  angel vine kissing ball
  willow branches
  mint plants
  thyme
  cilantro
  sage
  chives
dried/preserved
  river cane
  lichens
  reindeer moss
  mood moss
other
  chenille stem
  pan-melt glue
  dry foam
  honeysuckle wire
  lichen-covered Roman vase

1 Fill a lichen-covered urn with foam, and cover the foam with mood moss. Cluster olive branches into a topiary tree, and insert the stems into the center of the foam-filled pot.

2 Starting just beneath the tree's foliage, begin braiding several strands of twig garland around the woody stems, and continue down the length of the tree "trunk."

3 Place *Sedums* and *Echeverias* into the foam in groups around the base of the olive tree. Add trailing ivy on both sides of the container. Glue one olive atop the *Sedum*.

Peace Tree

Olive-laden branches are assembled into an elegant topiary.

A quartet of fruited olive branches — traditional symbols of peace — are masterfully clustered into a topiary tree and bound with a braid of twig garland, which contributes to a lifelike planted topiary presentation.

Surrounding the tree's trunk is a gathering of succulents, including a grand *Echeveria*, which establishes an intriguing focal point with the necessary visual weight to balance the skyward-pointing branches. Miniature French ivy, flowing from the succulent-covered base, adds dimension, further balancing the emphatic vertical lines.

Place this glorious olive tree in spacious entryways, on mantels and upon hearths throughout the warm summer months.

materials:
silk/permanent
olive branches
Echeveria
Sedum
miniature French ivy
twig garland
dried/preserved
mood moss
other
dry foam
hot glue
lichen-covered urn

Pitcher-Plant Tower

Butterflies and delicate plantings soften the lines of a *Sarracenia* sculpture.

1 Fill an urn with dry foam, and cover with moss. Swirl honeysuckle vine around the pot's rim in wreath formation, and pin the vine into the foam with "hairpins" made from heavy-gauge wire.

2 Assemble *Sarracenia* into a bunch, and insert the bunch into the center of the foam-filled urn. Place chamomile and fern plants into the foam near the base of the *Sarracenia* structure.

3 Add *Galax* leaves. Then, hot-glue monarch butterflies' wire stems into the foam, so they appear to be flitting about the design's base, and hot-glue another onto the *Sarracenia* bloom.

Flitting about a landscape of chamomile and royal fern, a happy trio of butterflies, on delicate wire stems that allow gentle movement, contribute to the botanical qualities of this pleasing composition. The florals, amid a brambly wooded base, grow as they would in nature, achieving a symbiotic balance through asymmetry.

A fourth butterfly, lighted upon one of the pitcher plant blossoms, is an unexpected surprise atop the sculptural formation, helping to emphasize the *Sarracenia* grouping's powerful vertical lines.

With its mostly monochromatic palette, this pretty presentation is versatile for home or office display and can remain in place throughout the summer months.

materials:
silk/permanent
   Sarracenia
   chamomile
   royal fern plant
   Galax leaves
dried/preserved
   honeysuckle vine
   mood moss
other
   monarch butterflies
   hairpin wires
   dry foam
   hot glue
   small urn

Grape Pretenders

Podded sprays and exotic florals replicate a stylish vessel's fruited motif.

1 Fill a vase with foam. Wind a *Eucalyptus* pod spray around the neck of the vase, just below the lip. Conceal foam with reindeer moss.

2 Insert pineapple lilies into the foam. Curl the ends of the twig garland by wrapping them around a pencil to simulate grape vine tendrils.

3 Insert a *Eucalyptus* pod spray next to the pineapple lilies, and bend the uppermost portion of the spray to form an arch that frames the other elements.

Selected to imitate the grape pattern on the impressive crackle-finish vase, a spray of berrylike *Eucalyptus* pods forms a bounteous collar, and another, arching above the design like a shepherd's crook, frames the composition and directs attention to the provocative pineapple lilies, with their recurved, tropical-fruitlike foliage, at the design's center. Twig garland, curled to resemble tangly grape vine tendrils, reinforces the fruited theme.

While this luscious decorative can elegantly enhance any home or office on its own, especially a credenza or side table, it would be endlessly dramatic in pairs atop a mantel, with two opposing pod-filled shepherd's crooks.

materials:
silk/permanent
 pineapple lilies
 Eucalyptus pod sprays
 twig garland
dried/preserved
 reindeer moss
other
 dry foam
 crackle vase

Gloriosa Grandeur

Just a few stems of an exotic-looking blossom create drama.

Cascading from within the bowl of an oversized cocktail-like vessel, the uncommon blooms of these exquisite *Gloriosa* lilies demonstrate that they possess enough glamour to be displayed monobotanically in a simple swirl.

Inside the stemmed glass container, which also could be used as a candleholder, the mechanics are equally simple yet dynamic; Asian honeysuckle vine is spun, en masse, inside the bowl, and the lilies' stems are tucked into the vine webbing.

Despite its grand proportions, this design would be absolutely stunning arranged in multiples, especially along the length of a contemporary table.

1 Swirl Asian honeysuckle vine around the inside of the container.

2 Insert *Gloriosa* lilies into the swirled vines at a shallow angle. Shape the lilies' stems to follow the contour of the container.

3 Tuck additional lily stems into the vines near the first insertion points to continue the spiraling line. Continue to shape the lilies in dynamic swirls.

materials:
silk/permanent
  Gloriosa lilies
dried/preserved
  Asian honeysuckle vine
other
  candleholder/bowl

Nature's Mechanics

Nests and willow orbs serve as armatures in this glorious composite.

Atop a quartet of berry-lined cylinder vases, a texturally diverse collection of botanicals is artfully woven together to create this wonderfully dynamic composite arrangement that would shine brilliantly in homes and offices with modern flair.

The contrast in textures, from rough and woodsy to sleek and smooth, along with the rhythm and visual movement established by the sinuous vines and flowing stems, capture attention and encourage extended gazing.

Including the gorgeous burgundy callas and captivating orange crown flowers, this design's ardent hues celebrate the warmth of summer, but the design will be equally dazzling during other seasons as well.

materials:

dried/preserved
crown flowers
Canella berries
curly willow balls
kiwi vine
bell pods
nests

silk/permanent
callas

other
glass cylinders

1 Clip *Canella* berries from stems, and drop them into the cylinder vases. Use enough berries to cover the base of each cylinder.

2 Cut a hole in the base of a nest, and insert sections of kiwi vine through the hole and into a vase. Insert more vines through a willow ball and into another vase. Repeat for the remaining vases.

3 Arrange bell cups and callas by threading their stems through the balls and nests, and position the stems inside the vases.

Three Times the Charm

This Asian-themed trio composes a singularly masterful accessory.

Three resplendent red cylinder vases, into which persimmon-hued bamboo and *Equisetum* in a complementary green are tightly wedged, compose a striking trio on their own. But when joined together in a single unit—accomplished by lacing additional bamboo horizontally through the vertical arrangements—and accessorized with florals and a shelter of copper wire, the group becomes a stunning composite that can grace the modern home or office.

While the arrangement's warm, rich hues embrace the ardor of summer, its complementary red and green color palette, accented by glittering gold, is appropriate through the holiday season.

1 String permanent orchid blossoms consecutively onto copper bullion wire to form a garland by wrapping the wire around each orchid's stem.

2 Cut bamboo into varying lengths, and wedge it, along with some *Equisetum*, tightly into the containers. Lace more bamboo horizontally through the vertical materials, connecting the designs.

3 Drop sand daisies into open bamboo ends. Entwine copper wire among the bamboo and sand daisies, for a sheltering effect. Repeat the technique using the wire-and-orchid garland.

materials:
dried/preserved
  sand daisies
  Equisetum
  burned bamboo
silk/permanent
  orchid blossoms
other
  copper bullion wire
  cylinder vases

45

Treasures of the Sea

Seashore finds are showcased in this ocean-themed accent.

Tropical seashores and salty ocean breezes are called to mind by this collection of aquatic "found" objects, which are glued onto wood picks and arranged atop foam secured inside a sandy-hued planter.

The mix of textural materials, including various shells and a starfish, is accented by wispy tendrils of sisal that echo the gentle movement of seaweed flowing with the tide. Globe thistles, with their prickly textures and watery ocean hue, are well-chosen enhancements that add subtle briny coloration to the neutral palette.

And representing sandy beaches or a pebbled ocean floor, white aquarium gravel is affixed to vines and branches and glued in place as a shelter for the oceanic finds.

1 Hot-glue seashells onto wood picks, and insert them into foam that extends about 3 inches above the container's rim. Tuck in clusters of sisal strands.

2 Hot-glue globe thistles among the shells to fill any voids.

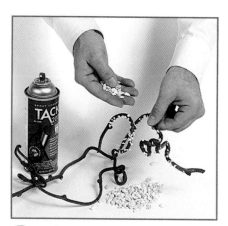

3 Spray bits of kiwi vine and branches with adhesive, and roll in aquarium gravel. Glue the branches atop the aquatic mound, and enwrap the materials with a few strands of sisal.

materials:

dried/preserved
  globe thistles
  sisal
  kiwi vine branches
other
  seashells
  starfish
  aquarium gravel
  wood picks
  spray adhesive
  plastic foam
  planter

Rabbit Repose

A showy Southern blossom brightens a bunny's peaceful resting place.

Relaxing in a bed of *Magnolia* foliage, assembled atop a bunch of dried China millet that is bundled into a sheaf, is a diminutive bunny, whose leafy concealment is bejeweled with a pristine white *Magnolia* blossom that is positioned in the center of the leaves like a brilliant medallion. Luxurious silk ribbon streamers, which flow from within the focal area, enhance the gardeny decorative with gentle movement and a sheeny golden hue that delicately complements the neutral palette without overpowering it.

Place this restful selection on coffee tables, sofa tables, buffets, credenzas and other types of lengthy tabletops in both homes and offices.

1 Bundle millet into a sheaf. Secure two clusters of *Magnolia* foliage, with leaves pointing in opposite directions, onto the center of the millet sheaf with waterproof tape.

2 Attach ribbon streamers to wired wood picks, and glue them into the leaf-enhanced millet bundle. Glue a large, open *Magnolia* blossom into the center of the leaves like a medallion.

materials:
silk/permanent
  Magnolias
  Magnolia foliage
dried/preserved
  China millet
other
  silk ribbon
  wired wood picks
  pan-melt glue
  waterproof tape
  rabbit

3 Dip the rabbit's paws into pan-melt glue, and nestle it into the bed of leaves atop the millet sheaf.

Layered Sheaves

Multisheaf wall or door décor artfully embraces summer.

Sheaves of bayou grass, cattails and rye are bundled into tiered layers to create this exquisite piece, which can hang on a wall or door from late summer through the Thanksgiving holiday.

Toward the base of this fabulous multi-sheaved hanging, a band of moss covers the outermost mechanics just beneath the tightly bundled rye, and, topped by a ring of sand daisy medallions, creates the primary focal point.

The uppermost sheaves, comprised of cattails and grasses decorated with a quartet of rare Lady Amherst feathers, composes a second focal point and draws visual attention from bottom to top.

materials:
dried/preserved
  sand daisies
  rye
  bayou grass
  giant cattails
  mood moss
  reindeer moss
other
  Lady Amherst feathers
  honeysuckle wire
  hot glue

1 Assemble grass into a fan-shaped bundle, and bind with honeysuckle wire. Place a cattail sheaf atop the grass, and bind again. Lay rye atop the sheaves, and bind it just beneath the grain heads.

2 Trim and glue a 4-inch band of mood moss around the grouping of sheaves just beneath the rye grains. Glue bits of reindeer moss beneath the moss band.

3 Hot-glue sand daisies into the space between the grain heads and the top of the mood moss band. Finish the design by tucking Lady Amherst feathers into the grasses.

Pocketful of Wild Grass

Marshy-looking materials are tamed with formal collars.

For both door and wall décor, a fabulous moss-lined wall pocket—the moss conceals the dry foam mechanic—is lavishly filled with a fan-shaped mass of wild grass, branches and feathers. Graceful swirls, achieved by gently curling the ends of the uncommon pheasant feathers, add energy and movement to the radiating materials. The untamed, marshy-looking grouping is then tailored with crisp collars of polished mahogany pods and preserved salal leaves.

While this sizeable pocket is ideal for interior walls (use in pairs like organic sconces) and doors, it can grace exterior doors as well, but wiring the foam in place and reinforcing insertions with glue is recommended.

1 Line a wall pocket with sheet moss, and tuck a brick of dry foam into the center of the moss-lined pocket.

2 Cut grasses and branches to a uniform length, and arrange them, along with the feathers, in a fan shape. Encircle the fan design with a collar of mahogany pods.

3 Insert rows of salal leaves into the moss-filled space between the pods and the wire basket's rim.

materials:
dried/preserved
  wild grass
  mahogany pods
  salal leaves
  birch branches
  sheet moss
other
  Lady Amherst feathers
  dry foam
  wall pocket

Tufted Collar

Great grains are beautifully enhanced with seasonal staples.

1 Trim millet stems to consistent lengths, and insert them, in bunches, into the dry foam in a fan shape.

2 Wrap a chenille stem around the end of a stick; dip into glue. Dab the glue onto bundles of foxtail grass and millet, and insert the bundles at the base of the millet fan in a crisscross manner.

3 Glue in pomegranates and pods in small groups among the foxtail and millet tufts. Fill in with quince slices and cinnamon-stick bundles.

Clustered around a vivid basil-hued fan of China millet, tufts of dried fall fruits and other materials impart a bountiful harvest feel, as well as autumnal color and textural intrigue, to complete this glorious creation.

The towering assembly of grains is placed into floral foam, the top inch of which extends above the container. In this space, foxtail grass and China millet bundles are inserted and then accessorized with the harvest gathering.

Due to its size, this offering should be displayed in expansive spaces, such as airy entryways, and atop large buffet and sofa tables. And with its collar of fruits, vegetables and spices, it would be suitable to grace sizeable islands in roomy kitchens.

materials:
dried/preserved
China millet
foxtail grass
pomegranates
quince slices
poppy pods
okra pods
cinnamon sticks
other
dry foam
pan-melt glue
planter

Gracious Greens

Grass, foliages and green-colored blossoms yield classic elegance.

Verdant groupings of materials, placed into a dry foam-filled tole vessel as single units, compose this classic creation that can grace many types of homes and offices.

Linear groups, such as the fan fern, are arranged into a modified inverted "T," where the vertical portion of the "T," formed by bayou grass clipped into a bristling bunch, is shorter than traditional line-mass "T" forms. Mass materials, such as pretty color-enhanced yarrow, fill out the center, forming a pleasing focal area. Faux branches and gracefully arching Lady Amherst feathers add energetic movement to the static "T."

Given this design's mostly monochromatic palette, it can accessorize nearly any interior color scheme throughout the year.

1 Clip bayou grass to a consistent length, and place into a foam-filled container in groups to form a small hedge.

2 Assemble fan fern into groups, and insert them into both ends of the dry foam block, forming a horizontal line.

materials:
dried/preserved
bayou grass
fan fern
yarrow
salal leaves
badam nuts
silk/permanent
faux branches
other
Lady Amherst feathers
dry foam
tole planter

3 Place faux branches around the bayou grass group. Add badam nuts, salal leaves and yarrow in groups into the center to create the focal area.

Down on the Bayou

Wild grasses sway amid rings of marshy-looking materials.

Tall blades of bayou grass form energetic lines in this elegant three-tiered sculptural piece that belies its simple construction.

Contrasting with the powerful dynamic vertical lines formed by the grasses, textural collars of *Sarracenia* and fan fern encircle the grassy fountain and add tremendous visual interest at the base. The fern fronds, which are clipped apart for individual placement, radiate from the central axis, adding horizontal balance to the upright materials.

Despite its height, this creative design is lightweight and can be utilized with containers of various sizes, and, given its neutral hues, affords numerous décor options, in homes and offices.

1 Using three bunches of bayou grass, form a thick bundle. Dip the ends into pan-melt glue, and wedge the glued bundle tightly into the container.

2 Cut *Sarracenia* stems to a uniform length. Dip each stem into pan-melt glue, and insert it, in collar formation, around the bayou grass.

3 Break or clip fan fern into individual fronds. Dip the fronds into pan-melt glue, and place them around the *Sarracenia* in haphazard placements that resemble ferns' natural growth.

materials:
dried/preserved
bayou grass
deluxe *Sarracenia*
fan fern
other
pan-melt glue
urn

Divergent Duo

Dissimilar barley and weeping willow combine for delightful décor.

Featuring a crisp, neatly ordered sheaf of barley positioned atop a loosely flowing bundle of weeping willow, this autumnal wall or door sheaf is a dichotomous union of tailored and free-flowing materials that proves to have harmonious results.

The two differing elements are unified by feathery fronds that radiate from the central binding point and ease the visual transition from the structured barley to the unstructured weeping willow. The fern, assembled in airy fans, also directs attention to the pair of bows, tied from two contrasting silk ribbons, that form the focal area.

For an even more untamed look, vertically clip some of the locks of willow to thin the foliage and expose some of the stems of the barley.

1 Assemble barley into a sheaf, and secure with wire. Bundle weeping willow, invert the bundle and wire it to the barley sheaf.

2 Tie bows from 2-inch and 4-inch silk ribbon. Secure the bows to a wired wood pick. Dip the pick into pan-melt glue, and insert it into the barley bundle.

3 Dip the end of each fern frond into pan-melt glue, and fill out the space between the willow and barley bundles, positioning the fronds so they radiate from the center of the silken bows.

materials:
dried/preserved
   barley
   fan fern
silk/permanent
   weeping willow
other
   cream silk ribbon
   dark gold silk ribbon
   wire
   wired wood pick
   pan-melt glue

53

1 Gather fountain grass into a group, and insert into the center of the foam-filled vase. Encircle the fountain grass with permanent branches cut to length, so they'll slightly overlap the grassy group.

2 Snip lilac stems short, so they'll extend about halfway up the branches. Insert them into the foam, completely encircling the previously arranged materials.

3 Group several stems of China millet together, and attach them to a wired wood pick. Arrange the millet, interspersed with durian, as a final collar.

Fall Phoenix

Permanent and dried materials erupt in flame-like sprays.

Like the phoenix, the mythical bird of the flames, this tiered composition rises from an umber bed of China millet and explodes in a fiery burst of fountain grass, imbuing its surroundings with new life.

Between the blazing millet, which is dotted with prickly durian, and the flaming fountain grass are smoldering permanent lilacs in a warm adobe hue and combusting branchlets, all of which are arranged in sequential tiers, evoking the floral bonfire.

The monochromatic palette, whose hot hues are desirable for autumn décor, are emboldened by the subdued green hues of the weathered milk-jug-shaped, pomegranate-embellished container, contributing to the burning effect.

materials:
silk/permanent
   durian
   lilacs
   branches
   fountain grass
dried/preserved
   China millet
other
   wired wood picks
   dry foam
   round vase with pomegranate
      handles

54

Bohemian Rhapsody

Carefully structured assembly relaxes with unconventional details.

Radiant Indian paint brush, crimson *Proteas*, and flame-tipped feathers cause this arrangement to glow with autumn's ardor. Arranged in sequential Biedermeierlike rings, with the materials placed in progressively taller zones, the composition resembles a fiery tiered starburst.

Yet with its wire-wrapped wooden vessel and prickly textures juxtaposed against soft feathery ones, this robust selection of dried materials has a somewhat rhapsodic, or improvised, "bohemian" character in which the orderly placement of materials is balanced by delightfully unexpected styling.

As a result, this design appeals to consumers of several different age levels and has many decoratives uses in the home.

1 Wrap the log cylinder with barked wire. Fill the cylinder with dry foam that extends about 3 inches above the container's rim.

2 Place the Indian paint brush around the foam's perimeter in ring formation. Add a ring of boxwood just inside the Indian paint brush and a circular mass of *Proteas* inside the boxwood.

3 Finish by inserting a ring of feathers into the foam between the boxwood and the *Proteas*.

materials:
dried/preserved
  Proteas
  Indian paint brush
  painted boxwood
other
  feathers
  dry foam
  barked wire
  log cylinder

1 Insert tall birch branches around the perimeter of a foam-filled urn. Tuck a bird's nest into the center of the branches.

2 Gather the birch branches together at their tips, and bind them with honeysuckle wire, forming a tall peak. Fill the center of the branchy "cage" with nature mix and other pods.

3 Wrap the remainder of the branch structure with honeysuckle wire to completely enclose it. Wedge short birch branches between the "cage" and the pot to create a birch collar.

Seussical Sculpture

Exotic botanicals are sheltered within a branchy cocoon.

With its pointed spire, reminiscent of a Dr. Seuss-created character, just a hint of whimsy is conveyed in this architectural construction that features a gathering of pods concealed within tall birch branches, which are wrapped in a cocoon structure.

The resulting composition, despite its fanciful touch—achieved by gathering the tips of the birch branches and wrapping them with natural-looking honeysuckle wire—has a decidedly formal air, and, with its overall neutral hues, seems suited for an African-themed space.

Given the design's height, weighting the vase is recommended to prevent toppling, especially for placement in high-traffic areas.

materials:
dried/preserved
 nature mix
 baobab pods
 birch branches
 bird's nest
other
 honeysuckle wire
 dry foam
 urn

Circular Bog

Wetlands vegetation is lavishly composed into a dynamic wreath.

Grand in both scale and presentation, this luxuriant wetlands-inspired wreath can beautifully embellish a large exterior door or an extravagant table, especially in a lodge-style home or woodsy retreat.

The marshy flora, whose lush, layered appearance belies the design's basic mechanics, are assembled atop a smilax wreath onto which bamboo and willow spheres are wired. The intricate orbs, into which stems are threaded, hold the materials in place. For outdoor use, glue or wire may be utilized for additional support.

Pheasant feathers, gently curled to maintain the wreath's circular rhythm, finish the composition with a natural avian flourish.

1 With lengths of honeysuckle wire, secure a total of six bamboo and willow balls atop the smilax wreath.

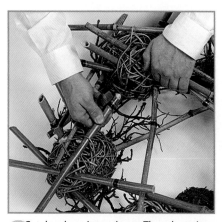

2 Cut bamboo into pieces. Thread a piece through one of the balls and into another, in a lacing manner, joining them together. Continue until all balls are connected and a grid is formed.

3 Insert stems of mahogany pods into the vine balls. Gently flex the cattail stems, and insert them into the structure. Finish with a few pheasant feathers.

materials:
dried/preserved
giant cattails
mahogany pods
burned bamboo
curly willow balls
bamboo balls
large smilax wreath
other
Lady Amherst feathers
honeysuckle wire

Worldly Gems

Exotic drieds are dynamically enhanced by curled plumage and vines.

1 Fill a compote with dry foam that rises 3 inches above the rim. Arrange pods in groups, and accessorize with balls and swirls of kiwi vine. Add *Proteas* in groups.

2 Between individual or group placements, tuck in bits of angel vine to fill gaps and add another textural element.

3 Lightly curl the pheasant feathers by running the blunt edge of a knife or scissors gently along the shafts. Finish the design by adding a "cage" of dynamic feather swirls.

Handsome swirls of feathers from the rare Lady Amherst pheasant, a seldom-found bird native to China and Burma, capture attention and direct eye movement to the diversity of materials sheltered within the feathery veil. The plumes' movement is echoed by twists of kiwi vine, which wind through the eclectic mix of pods, balls and *Protea* blooms. And tucked between the botanical groupings, wispy clusters of angel vine lend a delightfully unexpected texture.

The exceptionally masculine composition, which, with its neutral hues, has year-round appeal, would attractively enhance most spaces in a gentleman's home. It's also beautifully appropriate for formal office settings.

materials:

dried/preserved
jinga pods
baobab pods
monkey face pods
Proteas
bamboo balls
pintail feather ball
kiwi vine
angel vine
other
Lady Amherst feathers
dry foam
compote

Pod-Covered Topiary

Easy assembly is required.

1 Dip the end of a ready-made willow bundle into pan-melt glue, and wedge it tightly into a container.

2 Wrap honeysuckle garland around base of willow bundle, and nestle into container. Insert three wood picks into dry foam. Dip the picks into glue, and insert into top of willow bundle.

3 Arrange materials into the foam in a spherical shape, dipping the stems into pan-melt glue for added security. Fill any gaps with salal leaves and bits of angel vine.

With the help of a few design tools, intended to make product assembly quick and easy, completing this botanical topiary is a snap.

First, a willow bundle, used as a topiary "trunk," requires no assembly; it's already banded and is simply glued in place. And many of the pods are part of a designer assortment, sold with picks attached, so minimal labor is required. They're just placed into dry foam that is glued atop the willow bundle. Likewise, the vine accents— Asian honeysuckle vine at the base and bits of angel vine woven among the pods—are quick, beautifully appropriate accessories.

Recommend this for home and office display throughout autumn.

materials:
dried/preserved
austriaca cone
baobab pods
badam nuts
small *Proteas*
pod assortment
salal leaves
angel vine
Asian honeysuckle garland
willow bundle
other
wood picks
dry foam
pan-melt glue
urn

1 Fill a container with dry foam. Dip the base of a large gourd into pan-melt glue, and place the gourd atop the foam at an approximately 45-degree angle with the foam's surface.

2 Gather grains into monobotanical sheaves. Bind the stems with waterproof tape. Secure the sheaves, some inverted and some upright, into the foam using wood picks or hairpin wires.

3 Add rose hips, *Proteas* and foliage into the design in groups. Accessorize with kiwi vine. Loosely wind the berried garland around the lush composition.

Autumn Quintessence

Plentiful fall fruits are gathered into a zestful harvest centerpiece.

Brilliant hues, although sometimes uncharacteristic of drieds, shine brightly in this prismatic autumnal collection that reflects the season's richest palette.

The materials, like a bounteous harvest of sun-ripened fruits and sheaves of grain, spill over from within the large, heavy-laden vessel into which they're lavishly stored.

The effusive product placement, in which the wealth of elements is stacked and layered, increases depth and emphasizes textures, inviting extended gazing. As a result, this consummate fall piece, with its fruitful harvest theme, is perfect as a centerpiece on a Thanksgiving table as well as other autumnal meals and gatherings.

materials:
dried/preserved
  gourds
  Proteas
  China millet
  wheat grass
  salal leaves
  leaf acorn assortment
  kiwi vine
silk/permanent
  berried garland
  rose hips
other
  dry foam
  wood picks or hairpin wires
  waterproof tape
  pan-melt glue
  urn

Feathered Tussie-Mussie

Victorian charm meets with fashion flair.

1. Gather four bunches of star flowers into a bundle. Shape the bundled blossoms into a mound by patting the heads with your hand. Secure with waterproof tape.

2. Arrange a collar of ostrich feathers around the flowery mound, and secure the feathers with waterproof tape.

3. Enwrap the stems of the posy with ribbon, concealing the tape. Insert pearl-head corsage pins at an angle into the ribbon, forming an evenly spaced vertical column.

Fashionably collared by a fringe of gray ostrich feathers and detailed for display or for carrying with a wrapping of wired ribbon finished with a column of teardrop-shaped corsage pins, this nosegay of white star flowers is as appropriate for a bride as it is for a Victorian parlor.

The tussie-mussie can be customized with star flowers in a wealth of different hues to coordinate with wedding color schemes or home interiors, making it a versatile and adaptable design for both bridal parties and nostalgic decorators. In addition, the chic ribbon wrapping and periwinkle-colored pins can be easily modified to accessorize the selected star flower hues.

materials:
dried/preserved
dried star flowers
other
ostrich feathers
ribbon
waterproof tape
periwinkle corsage pins

Modern Geometry

A rounded design sits atop a square vase filled with vertical elements.

Delightfully unusual poppy pods are simply arranged in a mounded formation among deep-green *Galax* leaves whose color contrasts beautifully with the pale green of the *Equisetum*, which tightly fills the clean-lined square vase. The captivating lines formed inside the clear glass vessel add visual intrigue and direct attention to the basic pod and leaf formation that tops the container of hollow shoots.

In addition, the design's spherical shape echoes the unusual pods' rounded forms and develops a striking contrast with the square container, resulting in a modern-day aesthetic to accessorize today's contemporary interiors throughout fall or year-round.

1 Fill a square vase with *Equisetum*. Trim the green shoots to a height that is slightly taller than the container's rim. Save the trimmed bits of *Equisetum*, and wedge them tightly into the vase.

2 Insert three hyacinth stakes into a block of dry foam, and insert the other ends of the stakes into the midst of the *Equisetum*, which serves as the mechanics to hold the foam in place.

3 Apply steel picks to *Galax* leaves with a stemming machine. Arrange the leaves into the foam in a mound, covering the brick. Finish by inserting poppy pods, spaced evenly among the *Galax* leaves.

materials:
dried/preserved
  poppy pods
  Galax leaves
  Equisetum
other
  hyacinth stakes
  steel picks
  dry foam
  square glass vase

Hedged Roses

A work of art for transseasonal or year-round accessory.

Exhibiting rich crimson and orange hues, vibrant green foliage and moss accents, and a wealth of stimulating textures, this sublime centerpiece makes a compelling fall decorative that will transition seamlessly to Christmas. In fact, with its aesthetic qualities, this artful piece could grace formal tabletops throughout the year, and viewers will remain fascinated with its depth, colors and textures.

Among the most intriguing textures is the ethereal *Skimmia*, which is arranged in a hedgelike mass. The tufts result when the velvet roses are inserted into the hedge. A collar of berries and rose foliage, snipped from the lengthy stems, encircles the hedge and is fenced in by a striking twig garland.

1 Glue foam atop a pedestal bowl. Mound mood moss onto the foam, and wrap fencelike garland around the moss-covered foam.

2 Arrange *Skimmia* into the foam in a dense, hedgelike thicket. In symmetrical placements, insert rose blossoms into the *Skimmia* grouping, and add others around the perimeter.

3 Tuck reindeer moss between the flowers and twig fence. Insert berry clusters into the foam, so they fill the space between the top of the fencing and the rose blossoms.

materials:

silk/permanent
  velvet roses
  Skimmias
  berry sprays
dried/preserved
  mood moss
  reindeer moss
other
  twig garland
  dry foam
  pan-melt glue
  bowl on pedestal

Fruits of the Earth

Grass, flower and tree produce are gathered into a naturalistic vessel.

In this autumnal offering, amber grains surround a gathering of flower and tree fruits arranged inside a woodsy vessel, which, with its mossy rim, appears to have been recently collected from beside a timbered stream. The bright-green reindeer moss complements the ruddy hues of the fruits—poppy pods, mahogany pods and pomegranates—some of which are polished to a brilliant sheen. The trio of fruits, although arranged in a circular pattern, are selected at random, for a hand-gathered presentation.

Ideal for a rustic lodge, a mountain retreat or a timberland dwelling, this woodsy selection embraces fall's harvest bounty with organic flair.

1 Gather wheat grass into bundles, trim stems to 3 inches and add a steel pick to each bundle. Insert picked bundles into the foam at an angle to form a 4-inch-wide collar. Top the center of the foam with Spanish moss.

2 Arrange pomegranates and pods into the moss-topped foam by selecting either a pod or pomegranate at random and placing it in row formation just inside the wheat grass collar.

3 Hot-glue tufts of reindeer moss around the pot's circumference, between the pot's edge and the ring of wheat.

materials:
dried/preserved
- wheat grass
- pomegranates
- mahogany pods
- poppy pods
- reindeer moss
- Spanish moss

other
- steel picks
- dry foam
- hot glue
- woodlands container

1 Completely fill an oval bowl with dry foam, and line the perimeter with reindeer moss.

2 Trim sunflower stems to a few inches in length, and insert them into the foam, so the blossoms stand at or near the container's rim. Fill in with strawflowers.

3 Cut sweet anise into clusters, and tuck them into the foam around the sunflowers.

Faux Dried

Radiant fabric flowers imitate drieds.

Offering a wealth of home display options — on kitchen islands, dining tables, coffee tables and more — a harvest-inspired oval ceramic bowl contains a golden gathering of autumn blossoms that seem to have dried in the warm rays of an Indian summer sun. These flowers, however, are actually fabric, manufactured to replicate the textures and hues of dried and preserved florals.

To create the design, which has a natural, slightly haphazard composition, the largest materials — the sunflowers — are arranged first, and the smaller strawflowers are tucked in around them. Spiky sprays of sweet anise are added last to extend the dimensions and fill in open spaces.

materials:
silk/permanent
   dried-look sunflowers
   dried-look strawflowers
   sweet anise
dried/preserved
   reindeer moss
other
   dry foam
   oval container

65

1 Place a glass cylinder into the center of a smilax wreath. Form angel vine around the cylinder, and push the vines down, to fill the center of the wreath. Wire the vine to the wreath. Arrange materials.

2 Wire trios of quince slices onto wood picks, dip the picks into pan-melt glue and insert the picked trios into the wreath.

3 Bundle cinnamon sticks with honeysuckle wire, and attach the bundles to wood picks. Dip the picks into pan-melt glue, and insert the glue-covered picks into the arrangement.

Wreath of Plenty

The bounty of fall's harvest expressed in wreath form.

Assembled onto a large ready-made smilax wreath, the center of which is partially filled with angel vine, this elegant candlelit centerpiece could also adapt to serve as autumnal wall or door décor, minus the candle, of course. But whether displayed horizontally or vertically, this traditional form, with its abundant massing of fall's bounteous gifts, will beautify almost any space through the Thanksgiving holiday.

Because some of the materials are a bit weighty, additional reinforcement, along with glue, is recommended if the wreath is to be hung on a wall or door. Organic-looking wire, like honeysuckle wire, is a great choice, since hiding it is not necessarily required.

materials:

dried/preserved
large smilax wreath
angel vine
miniature Indian corn
pomegranates
quince slices
Canella berries
globe thistles
boxwood
cinnamon sticks
other
honeysuckle wire
wood picks
pan-melt glue
candle
glass cylinder

Fruited Tower

Autumn favorites display throughout the season in faux form.

1 Remove the bird from the stake, and insert the stake into a pot filled with mossed foam. Alternately impale pomander ornaments onto the stake.

2 Clip berry picks in half, and arrange them around the base of the fruitful tower. Cut *Coreopsis* stems to varying lengths, and insert them through the berries and into the foam.

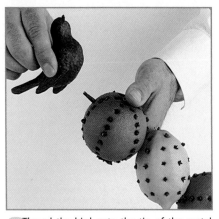

3 Thread the bird onto the tip of the metal stake. Twist a length of twig garland around the stake, just beneath the bird, and glue in a few berries and a single *Coreopsis* bloom.

Fresh citrus fruits, studded with cloves and star anise, are traditional fall icons that are often used as pomanders and allowed to dry during the season, infusing homes with spicy autumnal fragrances.

These faux versions, also decorated with cloves and anise stars, closely resemble their dessicating counterparts but are more versatile and offer inventive design options, as is demonstrated in this neatly assembled spire.

Around its base and at its peak, sun-drenched cranberries and amber *Coreopsis* blooms disguise mechanics and continue the harvest-hued palette. A winged visitor, on whose stake the fruits are impaled, rests quietly atop the piquant tower.

materials:

silk/permanent
  orange pomander ornaments
  lemon pomander ornaments
  field *Coreopsis*
  cranberry picks
  twig garland
dried/preserved
  mood moss
other
  bird stake
  pan-melt glue
  dry foam
  ceramic pot

Harvest Birdhouse

Fall florals and an avian abode festoon walls and doors in autumnal glory.

Imparting an almost tangible sense of the harvest season, with its leaf-winnowed trees and crisp autumn air, sprays of turning poplar foliage are woven into berried twig garlands and used to accessorize a decorative birdhouse, on which the home's little occupant is perched. The resulting fall-themed swag is glorious for ornamenting walls and doors throughout autumn.

A block of dry foam secured to the back of the birdhouse holds the materials in place, as well as a hand-crafted wire loop for hanging. Dried sand daisies, with their dark centers and bronzy amber hues, are affixed onto the leafy garlands and avian dwelling, adding depth and dimension.

1 Glue a block of dry foam to the back of the bird house. Insert twig garlands and leaf sprays into both ends of the foam.

2 Clip a bird onto the perch. Glue moss onto the clip to cover it. Glue sand daisy blossoms onto the birdhouse and onto the twigs.

3 Form a loop of wire as a hanger, and glue it into the top of the foam block. Glue leaves onto the foam to completely cover it.

materials:
silk/permanent
   poplar sprays
   twig and berry garland
dried/preserved
   sand daisies
other
   bird with clip
   birdhouse/windchime
   dry foam
   pan-melt glue
   reindeer moss

Pumpkin Patch

Vining fruits decorate doors and tables.

1 Wind the stem of the *Eucalyptus* pod spray around the stem of the rosemary topiary to join the two elements together.

2 At the end opposite the rosemary, twist pumpkin vine around entwined topiary and *Eucalyptus* stems. Clip sprigs of rosemary from the topiary's center. Accessorize the pumpkin.

3 Dip the base of the other pumpkin into pan-melt glue, and nestle it into the rosemary, affixing the fall fruit to the topiary's stem for maximum stability.

Whether hung on a door or laid upon a table as a deviceful elongated centerpiece, especially atop an autumn-inspired table runner in warm harvest hues, this intriguing composition of vining fall fruits offers a glimpse into a vegetatively crafted field of pumpkins with a pair of ripened specimens ready for picking.

At one end of the autumnal composition, the beauty of which belies its easy construction, one of the pumpkins is nestled into a bed of greenery—actually a rosemary topiary laid flat and entwined with sprays of *Eucalyptus* pods. A few snips of rosemary accessorize the other pumpkin, for a realistic field-planted effect.

materials:
silk/permanent
  pumpkins
  rosemary topiary
  Eucalyptus pod sprays
other
  pan-melt glue

69

Realistic Roses

Fabric roses mirror their fresh counterparts.

1 Fill a glass cylinder with birch branches. Clip the birch branches level with the container's rim.

2 Remove the lower foliage from the stems of the permanent roses. Gather the rose blossoms together in topiary form, and tie with ribbon. Insert the rose bunch into the branch-filled cylinder.

3 Clip a few roses to shorten their stems. Save and defoliate the clipped stems. Arrange both long- and short-stemmed roses into branches. Form the clipped stems into horseshoe shapes, and arrange into the branches.

Clearly man-made in its clustered topiary form yet with a discernably nature-made bramble look at the base, this striking two-part design conveys the illusion of fresh-cut flowers using lifelike fabric selections.

For visual intrigue, tension is established between the structured topiary shape, accented by sumptuous brown ribbon, and the free-form "wild rose" focal area at the base. Here, the dynamic rose placements add much-needed visual weight to balance the height of the topiary, whose foliage is mostly removed to emphasize the stem lines and to enhance the realism with visible thorns.

Roses are classic favorites, so recommend these for year-round home and office décor.

materials:
silk/permanent
   roses
dried/preserved
   birch branches
other
   ribbon
   square glass cylinder

Fruitful Harvest

Softened lines and a casual mass reflect fall's easy abundance.

In this bountiful fall accessory, two groups of budding branches, projecting upward inside an old-world vessel, form an airy, ethereal line while poppy pods, assembled into a bundle and placed perpendicularly to the branches, form a more definitive horizontal plane.

Keeping with the breezy character of the vertical branches, though, the horizontal line is softened by fluid berry sprays and fabulous roses that casually encircle the poppy pod stems like carefree climbers.

At the design's center, additional roses, guavas, pods and berries are massed into a harvest-gathered mound that overflows its container with blithe autumnal abandon.

materials:

silk/permanent
  roses
  guavas
  poppy pods
  pod sprays
  berry sprays
  twig spray
dried/preserved
  mood moss
  reindeer moss
  raffia
other
  hairpin wires
  pan-melt glue
  dry foam
  old-world container

1 Fill container with foam, and cover foam with reindeer moss. Tie a group of poppy pods with raffia to form a bundle. Lay the bundle atop the container, and pin into foam with hairpin wires.

2 Group a trio of twig sprays, and insert them vertically into the foam. Insert a second three-branch group parallel to the first. Arrange roses, guavas and pod sprays.

3 Encircle florals with berry sprays, and insert the berries' stems into the foam. Allow one spray to spill from the container, and finish with a few upright berry sprays.

Orchid Fountain

Sprays of exotic blossoms radiate from a bamboo-filled vase.

With transseasonal appeal from fall through the holiday season, multiple stems of efflorescing *Vanda* orchids are assembled into a dramatic Asian-inspired fountain that has a contemporary edge.

Contributing to the design's modern Oriental character is a bundle of cut bamboo, which serves as the mechanics. At the rim of the container, into which the bamboo bundle is wedged, orchids, *Proteas* and bits of smilax saved from other projects are tucked in among the canes. And the bamboo's hollow ends, accessed by cutting the canes just beneath the joints, are tiny receptacles for orchid sprays and individual *Protea* blossoms.

1 Cut bamboo into varying lengths, ensuring that each piece offers hollow space above the joint to allow floral stems to be inserted. Wedge the bamboo tightly into mouth of vase.

2 Tuck a few short-stemmed *Proteas* and orchids in among the bamboo. Add bits of smilax around the container's rim to fill the open space at the design's base.

3 Insert orchid and *Protea* stems into the open ends of the bamboo. If additional support seems necessary, secure the florals in place with glue.

materials:
silk/permanent
  Vanda orchids
  Proteas
  smilax leaves
dried/preserved
  burned bamboo
other
  crackle-finish vase with fruit

Dahlia Art

Long stems and negative space put exquisite florals on display.

1 Trim *Dahlia* stems to varying lengths, and, starting with the longest stems in the center and working outward to the shorter stems, position them in an urn filled with a column of dry foam.

2 Clip *Eucalyptus* pod sprays into smaller groups, and position them around the *Dahlia* stems.

3 Insert three short-stemmed *Proteas* at the center of the design, with the blooms resting atop the container's lip.

Luxuriant velvet *Dahlias*, in both bud and bloom forms in accordance with the principles of botanical design, are each purposefully positioned to create a simple yet breathtaking vertical fountain that, through its artfully sparse flower placements, maintains focus on the stunning blossoms, which are further emphasized by their slender stems.

Balancing the lofty floral sculpture requires a visually weighty base, accomplished in part by the generous proportions and deep hues of the crackle-finish vessel's grape motif. But visual balance is also achieved with clusters of *Proteas* and *Eucalyptus* pods assembled in a captivating focal area around the container's rim.

materials:
silk/permanent
velvet *Dahlias*
Proteas
Eucalyptus pod sprays
other
dry foam
crackle urn

Wintry Garden

Snowy blossoms flourish in a pretty planter box.

Resembling a lush garden of late-winter and early-spring florals, this profuse gathering of creamy-white *Irises*, *Viburnums*, *Magnolias* and tallowberries appears to be thriving in its charming planter. Adding to the composition's vegetative realism, the blooms point upward, as they would in nature, as if seeking the sun's warm rays. And a botanical influence is also evident, since the *Irises* are present in both bud and full bloom.

Especially with the addition of the reddish rose hips, which evoke a holiday feel, this creation is appropriate during December. But since the most of the flowers featured are traditional springtime bloomers, it can be displayed through early spring.

1 Arrange clusters of tallowberries among *Magnolias* in a foam-filled planter. Bend one of the clipped *Magnolia* stems into a "U" shape, and insert each stem end into the foam for added texture.

2 Gently flex the *Iris* stems into a shape that resembles the fresh flower in its natural growth patterns. Add *Irises*, as well as *Viburnums*, rose hips and other materials, into the design.

3 Tuck bits of angel vine among the blossoms, particularly around the base, for a grassy, vegetative feel.

materials:
silk/permanent
  Irises
  Viburnums
  Magnolias
  tallowberries
  rose hips
  wild grass
dried/preserved
  sable palm
other
  dry foam
  planter

Collared Sheaf

Dual collars encircle a grand assembly of grains.

1 Assemble rye into a large bundle, and gently twist to form a shock. Bind with honeysuckle wire. Glue clipped *Sarracenia* blooms onto grain bundle beneath the grain heads, hiding the wire.

2 Using red wire, secure *Canella* berries into a garland. Wrap the berry garland around the shock, just beneath the *Sarracenia* blooms. Fasten the ends together with red wire.

3 Tie a band of raffia, with a loose knot, around the gathering, between the berry garland and the *Sarracenia* collar.

Eight bunches of rye extravagantly compose this massive shock of grains while two bunches of intriguing *Sarracenia* encircle the grains to form a collar. Beneath the *Sarracenia*, the sheaf, which is bound with honeysuckle wire, is enwrapped with a decorative tie of raffia that conceals the wire binding. And just beneath the raffia twist, a ring of ruby *Canella* berries forms a bold collar and an eye-catching focal area.

The materials, along with the neutral hues intercepted by the vivid sanguine ring, lend themselves to both Thanksgiving and Christmas display, making this a versatile, transseasonal selection that could be placed in homes and offices in early autumn and remain through the end of the year.

materials:
dried/preserved
  rye
  Sarracenia
  Canella berries
other
  raffia
  honeysuckle wire
  red wire
  pan-melt glue

Framed Flowers

Organic additions dress a ready-made amaryllis plant for the holidays.

Ready-made floral designs and potted plants, whether fabric or dried, are tremendous time savers, and, like this gorgeous ready-made potted amaryllis, are radiant on their own, with no ornamentation required. But they're also wonderful for use as feature elements in customized designs, in part so florists' ready-made offerings are differentiated from those of their competitors.

Here, a luxurious velvet selection, sold in a weathered pot topped with a bit of faux moss, is glued into a bird's nest and framed by an arch of birch branches. Additional birch twigs, glued atop the pot in a crisscross manner, direct eye movement from the beaming blossoms to the aged pot and its organic base.

1 Glue two long birch branches into a bird's nest. Glue a second pair of branches opposite the first. Gather the ends of the branches into an arch, and bind with honeysuckle wire.

2 Dip the base of the amaryllis' pot into pan-melt glue, and insert the pot into the center of the nest, inside the branchy frame.

3 Cut thick birch branches into 5-inch twigs, and glue them atop the amaryllis' pot in a crisscross manner.

materials:
silk/permanent
  velvet potted amaryllis plant
dried/preserved
  bird's nest
  birch branches
other
  honeysuckle wire
  pan-melt glue
  hot glue

Winter's First Frost

Ice-laden branches replace twinkling lights on this woodsy creation.

1 Gather birch into a bundle, and insert it into a plastic-foam-filled pot that is accessorized with angel vine. Bind the tips of the branches with honeysuckle vine, and trim the tops evenly.

2 Assemble sweet huck into inverted bundles, and attach each bundle to the birch "trunk" with a rubber band.

3 Tightly coil honeysuckle wire around the top of the inverted sweet huck, to completely conceal the rubber bands.

Sweet huck branches, available in bunches like these that are glistening with a sparkling layer of frost, are assembled into a wintry woodlands tannenbaum that can bedeck a country home or modern office with equal flair and beauty.

In fact, since this tree lacks ornaments and holiday trim, and is assembled in an icy blue pot, it has a distinctively winter theme rather than an affiliation with a religious holiday; as a result, it's ideal for offices and other public settings.

For home display, recommend it in pairs for rustic mantels or assemble it in a larger scale for entryways and even great rooms, as an alternative to the traditional pine.

materials:
dried/preserved
  frosted sweet huck
  birch branches
  angel vine
other
  honeysuckle wire
  plastic foam
  ceramic pot

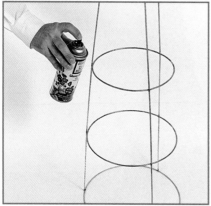

1 Spray the tomato cage with black paint. Shorten the cage's "legs," so it will fit in the pot, by snipping them with wire cutters or tin snips. Insert the cage into a pot filled with plastic foam.

2 To disguise the cage, secure groups of birch branches to each of the wires, starting with the vertical and continuing to the circular. Attach the branches with honeysuckle wire.

3 Arrange noble fir into foam. Assemble the "basket" for holding the cones by inserting branches horizontally, in a crisscross manner, onto the center ring of the cage. Embellish the basket with berries, and fill with frosted cones.

Christmas Cage

Woodland materials are expertly assembled in an elaborate topiary.

Rising from a snow-dusted thicket of preserved noble fir, a birch-branch framework, embellished with a berried garland, holds a frosty collection of winter-flocked cones.

The secret to this bilevel masterpiece is in its ingenious base—a tomato cage. The cone-shaped wire structure, available at most garden centers and nurseries, provides an instant armature to which the woody branches are attached. The red berries are swirled around the top of the cage, which is packed with an abundance of the wintry cones.

This innovative, two-tier composition, with its organic inspiration, is ideal for country or lodge-style interiors.

materials:
dried/preserved
noble fir
birch branches
large pine cones
silk/permanent
berry garland
other
honeysuckle wire
gloss black spray paint
tomato cage
plastic foam
lattice urn

Swirl Cone

A bedecked topiary makes a sweet treat for the Christmas season.

1 Cut a bundle of birch branches to 8 inches in height. Dip the bundle into pan-melt glue, and insert it into a foam-filled pot topped with moss. Glue a foam cone atop the branches.

2 Arrange boxwood and mood moss in swirls around the cone. Glue wood picks into the pomegranates, and starting at the top, insert the fruits between the moss and berries.

3 Use hairpin wires to secure *Canella* berry clusters onto the decorated foam cone.

Red and green fruits, arranged in spirals around a foam cone, make a striking yuletide decorative that would graciously welcome guests in an entryway or would be stunning in pairs on a mantel.

The mood moss and boxwood are well-chosen greenery, since, with their fringy textures, they imitate the foliage of a coniferous shrub. The "greens" are arranged onto the cone first in spiraling bands, and swirls of berries and pomegranates are arranged later, following the same dynamic lines.

Marking swirls onto the cone before decorating will help maintain the clean, distinctive bands. And during assembly, step back periodically to check the pattern.

materials:
dried/preserved
   pomegranates
   Canella berries
   mood moss
   boxwood
   birch branches
other
   hairpin wires
   plastic-foam cone
   dry foam
   pan-melt glue
   square pot

Wild Apples Tamed

Deliberately un-wild assembly contrasts with a primitive nest.

1 Assemble branches in a foam-filled vase to create a "trunk." Cut and remove the center of the nest, creating a wreathlike form. Insert the tree "trunk" into the nest opening, and slide the nest onto the vase.

2 Dip a plastic-foam sphere into pan-melt glue, and affix atop the birch branch "trunk."

3 Glue wild apples onto the plastic-foam sphere, and glue bits of reindeer moss in between the apples to conceal the foam.

Hearkening back to the manicured geometries of formal European gardens, topiary forms are widely coveted among many nature-loving cultures. Here, the most common of these shaped creations is interpreted with punctilious placements of mosses and holiday-red-infused wild apples.

But what is uncommon about this inventive topiary is the inverted pine-needle nest base from which the apple-covered orb emerges. Juxtaposed against the slightly untamed nest, the precisely ordered sphere's refined character is emphasized.

Most attractive in pairs, simple decorative statements like this one are at home in both contemporary and traditional environments.

materials:
dried/preserved
   wild apples
   birch branches
   nest
   reindeer moss
other
   plastic-foam sphere
   dry foam
   pan-melt glue
   vase

1 Lay a permanent *Magnolia* leaf wreath atop a foam-filled pot. Place a bundle of tall branches into the wreath's center, and press the bundle into the foam.

2 Shape *Iris* stems, foliage and blooms into lifelike poses, and insert the flowers' stems into the center of the topiary "trunk."

3 Slide the *Magnolia* leaves up the branchy "trunk" until it fits tightly at the base of the *Iris* blossoms. Glue wood picks to pomegranates, and glue the pomegranates into the wreath.

Topiary Fountain

Branches spray from within a leaf-wrapped *Iris* topiary.

A grand collection of fabric *Irises*, in a striking reddish hue, take center stage in this captivating topiary, which utilizes a *Magnolia* leaf wreath, accessorized with pomegranates, as a binding element. Erupting from within the *Iris* bundle is a fountain of the slender ends of tall birch branches, the lower ends of which encircle the flowers' stems and form the topiary "trunk."

With the incorporation of reds into the mostly brown color palette, this statuesque piece could decorate homes, in singles or in more impacting pairs, starting in fall and can remain on display through the Christmas season.

materials:

dried/preserved
  pomegranates
  birch branches
  moss
silk/permanent
  Irises
  Magnolia leaf wreath
other
  dry foam
  wood picks
  pan-melt glue
  pot

Gifts of the Orient

Bamboo and wire webbing support these glorious orchids.

1 Glue a saucer to the base of a clay pot. Dip a plastic-foam sphere into pan-melt glue, and secure it inside the clay pot, so about half of the sphere is exposed above the pot's rim like a mound.

2 Cut bamboo to 16 equal lengths. Space eight of them evenly around the pot's perimeter; place the remainder at angles with the first. Glue wild apples onto the foam, and fill gaps with moss.

3 Bind bamboo at cross points with red bullion wire. Cut more in random lengths, and bind to build a free-form armature. Wrap the wire around and across to form a web. Arrange orchid stems through the top of the web.

Several stems of exquisite fabric *Phalaenopsis* orchids, as magnificent and impressive as the fresh versions, are showcased in this Asian-themed holiday decorative, which features a striking web of luminous red wire wrapped onto an intricate free-form bamboo armature.

The orchid stems, laden with a wealth of buds and blooms, tower above a mossy landscape paved with ruby-red wild apples, creating, along with the webbed armature, three distinct areas of visual interest.

While its Asian inspiration is unmistakable, this creative composition could be at home in a variety of settings and could grace almost any tabletop in homes and offices.

materials:
dried/preserved
  wild apples
  burned bamboo
  reindeer moss
silk/permanent
  orchid sprays
other
  red bullion wire
  plastic-foam sphere
  pan-melt glue
  clay pot and saucer

Biedermeier Bowl

An oversized bowl is lavishly filled with fruitful concentric rings.

Rings of burnished red fruits, with subtle green hues at the top and base, are assembled into a beautifully structured mound that, with its ordered, Biedermeier-influenced style, is a fabulous holiday enhancement for traditional décors. And, whether used for formal dining or to adorn tabletops in other areas of the home, this punctilious composition would be exquisite paired with sleek tapers and other types of candles.

Although the hints of green, incorporated with preserved salal leaves and an Asian honeysuckle garland, enliven the ruddy hues and obviously invoke the Christmas spirit, this elegant arrangement could remain in place year-round.

1 Fill a large urn with two bricks of dry foam. Form Asian honeysuckle garland into a wreath, and lay the wreath onto the container's rim.

2 Create a ring of *Canella* berries by inserting their stems into the sides of the foam bricks, positioning them so the berry clusters rest atop the vine wreath.

3 Add a ring of pomegranates in a circumference that is slightly smaller than the berry ring. Fill the design's center with preserved salal leaves. Arrange poppy pods among the leaves.

materials:
dried/preserved
  Canella berries
  pomegranates
  burnt oak poppy pods
  salal
  Asian honeysuckle garland
other
  wood picks
  dry foam
  pedestal bowl

Linear Radiance

This formal line design represents the elegance of Christmas to a "T."

1 Lay twig sprays into a container in two sheaf-like groups, so the stems form an armature inside the vase and each group of buds protrudes from opposite sides of the container.

2 Bundle amaryllises, so the blooms form a rounded mound, and bind them with wire. Insert the bundled stems into the center of the vase, threading them through the branchy armature.

3 Insert *Canella* stems into the branch structure inside the vase. Allow most berry sprays to spill over the edge of the vase, but position some to follow the horizontal lines of the branches.

Two lines, one formed by horizontal branches and effluent *Canella* berries and the other by efflorescent amaryllises, converge perpendicularly in a spherical vase, composing an "interpretive" inverted "T," which features an atypically long horizontal line and a flourishing vertical line. Despite its interpretive departures from strict inverted "T" compositions, this exquisite creation possesses the elegance and formality usually associated with traditional line designs.

While visually enticing, the lines are also functional. The branches form an armature into which the materials are arranged, and the topiarylike mound of amaryllises echoes the shape of the reedy vessel.

materials:
silk/permanent
  mini velvet amaryllises
  twig spray
dried/preserved
  Canella berries
other
  wire
  reed vase

Iconic Groupings

Traditional holiday elements are combined in a sublime centerpiece.

Luscious red berries, berried holly, pine cones and gorgeous red amaryllises—all unmistakable icons of the holiday season—are assembled together in this splendorous centerpiece in dramatic groupings.

The amaryllises, with their captivating florescences, add tremendous weight to one side of the composition while visually lighter materials, such as the cones and berries, attempt to counterbalance the massive blooms. The asymmetrical balance lends an undisturbed, nature-inspired feel to the arrangement, which is ideal to accessorize tabletops for semi-formal holiday festivities.

Due to the urn's open lattice styling, moss, tucked between the dry foam and the container as a camouflage, finishes the design.

1 Insert a bunch of cranberries near the rim of a foam-filled urn. Insert another bunch directly across from the first. Place bunches of berried laurel between the two cranberry groups.

2 Place amaryllises into the foam on one side of the container to form a large group.

materials:

silk/permanent
  velvet amaryllises
  cranberry picks
  holly sprays
  berried laurel
dried/preserved
  austriaca cones
  reindeer moss
  angel vine
other
  dry foam
  lattice urn

3 Place cones into the foam on the opposite side of the container to form another large group. Finish by weaving wisps of angel vine among the materials.

Hidden Treasures

A well-planned mass design fulfills fall and Christmas décor needs.

1 Add a "pick" to a bundle of cinnamon sticks by wrapping honeysuckle wire around a plant stake. Secure the plant stake to the cinnamon bundle by wrapping the vine around the sticks.

2 Wire trios of quince slices together onto wood picks, and insert them into the arrangement.

3 Run the dull edge of a knife up the back side of the feather to add a gentle curve.

Lavish gatherings of materials are hallmarks of Thanksgiving and Christmas designs, and a masterful arrangement could serve both holidays with equal elegance.

The fact is beautifully demonstrated in this dynamic centerpiece, which includes seasonless vines, feathers and quince slices as well as a profusion of holiday staples. The resourceful combination of elements is key to the design's flawless transition from Thanksgiving to the Christmas season.

For extended display, the natural motion of the veiling feathers and vines encourages viewers to continually examine the static mass of treasures within.

materials:

dried/preserved
Canella berries
quince slices
strobus cones
kiwi vine
cinnamon sticks
silk/permanent
fir
sugar pine
other
feather balls
Lady Amherst feathers
wired wood picks
honeysuckle wire
plant stake
tin planter

Classic Example

A traditional centerpiece captures the spirit of the Christmas season.

1 Fill the urn with dry foam, and cover the foam with a layer of mood moss. Arrange miniature *Gladioli* into the foam to create horizontal lines.

2 Add snapdragons and *Protea* pines to begin forming the mass. When inserting the pines, gather the branches into a small cluster, and insert the stems all at once.

3 Thread the wire from a wood pick through each ornament hanger, and twist the wire tightly to secure. Insert the pick on each glass ball ornament into the center of the design.

Composed in a symmetrical horizontal triangle, this divine traditional mass arrangement features an exquisite gathering of fine permanent seasonal materials in an engaging complementary color harmony. As a result of its iconic elements and classic styling, this magnificent centerpiece represents the very quintessence of the season.

Miniature *Gladioli* and chokecherry branches are used masterfully to create the horizontal lines while berried holly and luxuriant velvet roses and snapdragons form the central mass. At the design's center, the focal point is comprised of a pair of luminous scarlet ball ornaments, completing the consummate holiday centerpiece.

materials:
silk/permanent
  miniature *Gladioli*
  velvet roses
  velvet snapdragons
  holly sprays
  chokecherry branches
  Protea pine
dried/preserved
  mood moss
other
  glass ball ornaments
  wired wood picks
  dry foam
  urn

Here Comes Santa Claus

Novel accessories add lighthearted cheer to idyllic collections.

Prancing into town mounted on a noble reindeer steed, this festive St. Nick, heralding the Christmas season, lends a hint of holiday whimsy to an opulent yet organic-looking centerpiece intended for capacious tabletops.

The deer and its jolly rider, which are a single unit with an attached baluster, are glued onto dry foam inside a grand bowl and arrayed with a halcyon mix of woodsy faux elements, including ravishing red berries and several coniferous greens, that appear to have been gathered from a timbered dale. Among the most important are long needle pine, which extends the proportions and, with its wispy bunches, visually lightens the substantial Santa-driven deer.

1 Fill the bowl with blocks of dry foam, and, using pan-melt glue, adhere the Santa-and-deer baluster atop the foam.

2 Arrange pine needles, cypress and seeded *Eucalyptus* into the foam. Wrap berry garland around the baluster base, and entwine its berried branches with the greenery.

3 Thread the wire from a wood pick through each ornament hanger, and twist the wire tightly against the wood pick to secure. Insert the picks into the design.

materials:
silk/permanent
- long needle pine
- berry garland
- seeded *Eucalyptus*
- cypress

other
- red glass balls
- wired wood picks
- pan-melt glue
- dry foam
- Santa on reindeer with baluster
- bowl

Fruited Topiary

Red cranberries and a pineapple topper distinguish a leafy cone.

1 Clip grape leaves from their branches. Starting at the base of the cone, pin on velvet leaves in overlapping layers. Position the consecutive leaf layers to conceal the pins on the previous layers.

2 Glue the pineapple into the top of the leaf-covered cone. Accessorize the pineapple's base with berries, pine and reindeer moss. Shape the pineapple foliage for a natural appearance.

3 Fill an urn with dry foam, and glue the leaf-covered cone atop the foam. Conceal the foam with needle pine and cascading berry sprays. Randomly glue bits of reindeer moss between the leaves.

Symbolizing hospitality—generous and cordial welcomes into pleasant home environments—the pineapple, despite its tropical heritage, is absolutely appropriate to top a gracious yuletide topiary. This one, positioned in a grand Roman urn, features a foam cone layered with gold-edged velvet leaves that are pinned, rather than glued, for dimension and to emphasize their soft textures. Cascading cranberries and boughs of needle pine complete the holiday theme.

In the South, pineapples are used as architectural details, signifying that those who enter will be warmly received. Therefore, this exquisite piece is ideal for placement in entryways as well as on hearths and mantels.

materials:
silk/permanent
 pineapple
 velvet grape leaves
 cranberry picks
 needle pine
dried/preserved
 reindeer moss
other
 pins
 dry foam
 plastic-foam cone
 hot glue
 pan-melt glue
 Roman vase

Stacked Tree

Scarlet berries and a tiny tannenbaum combine in a treelike decorative.

Nested pots, overflowing with lavish berry collars, are crowned with a miniature pine tree to complete this artistic alternative to the traditional tabletop-size Christmas tree.

The diminutive pine is adorned with a stylish finial-like topper, and additional berries, snipped from a single spray, are glued into the tiny tree as seasonal trim, repeating the red hue and ensuring a harmonious visual transition from top to bottom.

Because of its size and shape, which is somewhat reminiscent of a mountain pine, this holiday accent offers versatility in its placement and can be used to spread Christmas cheer throughout the home, but it would be especially impacting in pairs on mantels and credenzas.

1 Fill the smaller pot with dry foam, and top it with moss. Fill the larger pot with foam that extends 2 inches above the pot's rim. Dip the base of the small pot into glue, and affix it atop the foam.

2 In both pots, assemble berry sprays into lavish collars, but in the small pot, leave the foam's center open. Insert the trunk of the miniature tree into the center of the topmost pot.

3 Snip off the end of a finial-like drop ornament, and glue the ornament onto the peak of the miniature tree.

materials:

silk/permanent
   miniature pine tree
   cranberry picks
other
   red drop ornament
   pan-melt glue
   mood moss
   dry foam
   set of two graduated pots

Potted Wreath

Showcase the ubiquitous holiday favorite atop a stylish vessel.

1 Fill a container with dry foam that extends about 2 inches above the rim. Glue heavy-duty stakes into the wreath, and insert into the foam.

2 Secure strobus cones onto the smilax wreath. Using pan-melt glue, apply wood picks to pomegranates, and place them among the cones.

3 Add cranberry picks among the pomegranates and cones. Finish with foliated pepperberries by inserting the stems into the wreath and tucking the berries and foliage around the cones.

Wreaths are popular decoratives throughout the year, but at no time are they more in demand than at Christmas. Yet for those whose spaces, whether door, wall, mantels or otherwise, are not conducive to holiday wreath display, potted versions are ideal alternatives. They can be placed upon various types of tables for seasonal home or office décor and can effectively be scaled down to suit even the smallest tables.

This version of the venerable holiday decorative, assembled onto a smilax wreath form, features a swirling collection of fruits, cones and foliage. Due to the wreath's size, a weighted pot, large stakes and heavy-duty dry foam are required for stability.

materials:
dried/preserved
  pomegranates
  strobus cones
  smilax wreath form
silk/permanent
  pepperberries
  cranberry picks
other
  bamboo stakes
  wood picks
  pan-melt glue
  dry foam
  vase

Pocketed Wreath

Amaryllises and pepperberries pair with a versatile accessory.

Positioned atop an elegant wall pocket, this berry-encrusted wreath, assembled on a ready-made faux spruce base, is bedecked with two glorious clusters of luxuriant velvet amaryllises for a truly breathtaking Christmas display. The ravishing scarlet blossoms are grouped for maximum impact, and hanging *Amaranthus*, glued into the wreath at the base, flank the wall pocket and replace traditional ribbon streamers.

Although the wall pocket appears to be joined to the wreath, they are actually two distinct pieces. Therefore, the pocket, whether inside or outside the home, can remain in place while the wreath is simply replaced for each new season.

1 Using pan-melt glue, secure pepperberry garland atop a ready-made spruce wreath. Glue in salal leaves sporadically around the wreath.

2 Dip stems of amaryllises into pan-melt glue, and cluster the blossoms at the top of the wreath and at its base.

3 Hang a wall pocket onto a door. Position the wreath above the pocket, so the wreath and wall pocket appear to be a single unit.

materials:
silk/permanent
  velvet amaryllises
  Amaranthuses
  salal leaves
  spruce wreath
  pepperberry garland
other
  pan-melt glue
  wall pocket

92

Woodlands Wreath

Gilded leaves and berries highlight a woodsy cone decorative.

1 Glue wood picks to pine cones, and glue the cones onto a smilax wreath at various angles.

2 Spray permanent berries with gold paint, and allow to dry. Glue them onto the smilax wreath when dry.

3 Add bell cups to the cone-and-berry-covered wreath. Fill in with gold salal leaves and frosted preserved cedar. Tie a bow, affix it onto a wood pick, and glue the pick into the wreath.

An assortment of cones, some frosted, some painted and some in their natural hues, along with burnt oak bell cups, abundantly comprise this organic wall, door or tabletop selection. The wealth of cones, in their various brown tones, are accented by lustrous gilded leaves and berries as well as strategically placed preserved cedar, which has a sparkling frosty finish. Completing the predominantly brown-toned palette is a luxurious chocolate ribbon, the streamers of which are artfully woven among the botanicals.

This seasonal treasure, with its appealing textures and rich warm hues, can decorate a variety of spaces for the holidays but is a natural fit for country homes and lodges.

materials:
dried/preserved
austriaca cones
Protea flats
frosted pine cones
bell cups
frosted preserved cedar
smilax wreath
gilded salal leaves
silk/permanent
berries
other
gold spray paint
brown ribbon

Door Tassel

Sections of traditional Southern materials welcome visitors.

1 Assemble hanging fir into a fringy bundle, and wire the stem ends together. Secure pine cones, in groups of two, onto the bare ends of the fir stems.

2 Glue bits of boxwood around the pine cones pairs, filling the midsection of the design with greenery.

3 Layer *Magnolia* leaves atop the cone-enhanced tassel, and bind leaf stems to the bundled fir stems with honeysuckle wire. Top with a multiloop bow.

Imbued with a sense of the Old South, a collection of holiday evergreens, enhanced with *Magnolia* foliage and strobus cones, forms a charming swag that resembles a tassel.

Topped with a looping bow of wired ribbon, the expertly crafted swag is composed in widening, tassel-shaped layers, with the small mass of ocher *Magnolia* foliage—from the traditional southern blossom—at the top, followed by a section of preserved boxwood and strobus cones. The final layer comprises a gathering of hanging fir, the fringy dimensions of which complete the tassel effect.

However, assembly occurs in reverse order beginning with the faux fir, to which the other materials are attached, either with pan-melt glue or honeysuckle wire.

materials:

silk/permanent
   Magnolia leaves
   hanging fir
dried/preserved
   strobus cones
   painted boxwood
other
   honeysuckle wire
   ribbon
   pan-melt glue

Wintry Swag

Snow-clad door adornment warmly greets guests.

Assembled atop a ready-made flocked balsam swag in a teardrop shape, this frosty door piece, customized with a profusion of additional frosted and unfrosted materials, makes for anything but a chilly reception.

Instead, dark berries and soft feathers warm the bedecked teardrop, which can adorn interior walls as well. Iced *Lunaria*, or money plant, is also glued in, imitating the teardrop shape. Woven among the frosted balsam, the *Lunaria* adds an ethereal quality.

Rather than a bow and ribbon streamers, a dazzling mounded sheaf of dried star flowers, wired onto the swag base, is accented by the pine cones and brilliant *Magnolias* to serve as a grand accent detail.

materials:
silk/permanent
 Magnolias
 iced *Lunaria*
 cranberry picks
 privet berries
 branches
 flocked balsam teardrop
dried/preserved
 star flowers
 frosted white-pine cones
other
 feathers
 wire
 pan-melt glue

1 Gather star flowers into a sheaf, and form the dried blossoms into a tight mound by cupping them with your hand. Secure the star flower bundle with wire, and attach to a decorated swag.

2 Snip a pair of *Magnolia* blooms from their stem, and dip each into pan-melt glue. Affix the blooms onto the star flower bundle, covering the wire binding.

3 Assemble two groups of black feathers into fans, and secure them with wire. Dip the feather fans into glue, and tuck them into the swag, on either side of the star flower mound.

1 Enhance the ready-made wreath with guavas, silver dollar sprays and twig garland. To add iced pine cones, dip their bases into pan-melt glue, and tuck them into the greenery.

2 Snip rose stems to just a few inches in length. Dip the shortened stems into pan-melt glue, and insert them into the wreath.

3 To form the beaded streamers, thread each bead garland through a section of twig garland. Loosely knot each bead garland around a twig "fence post" to secure.

Blue Christmas

Snowy materials accent a cool blue base.

With this opulent door and wall adornment, composed on a ready-made wreath complete with an abundance of materials in a range of beryllic hues, a blue Christmas is actually a joyous occasion.

The lavish base, which features natural pine cones, dusty miller, *Eucalyptus* seeds and pods and a profusion of coniferous greens, requires little embellishment, but for a richness befitting the season, velvet roses, frosted cone ornaments and transparent silver dollar sprays are tucked amid the wintry elements.

Woven into the wreath is a fencelike garland from which flows glittering beaded garland, replacing traditional ribbon streamers.

materials:
silk/permanent
blue Christmas wreath
velvet roses
guavas
silver dollar sprays
iced pine cone ornaments
other
twig garland
bead garlands
pan-melt glue

Starry Swag

A decorated garland imitates a spiral topiary for wall or door placement.

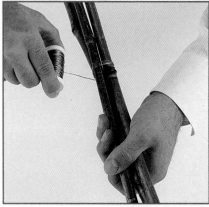

1 Wire three bamboo canes together to form a support for the garland.

2 At one end of the bamboo support, enwrap the canes with one of the garland's branches. Spiral the garland around the bamboo, and continue to secure to canes with branches.

3 Dip snowballs' stems into pan-melt glue, and insert them into the pine garland. For stars, dip one point into glue, and tuck the stars into the garland. For glass balls, dip the tops into glue, and affix them to the swag.

Potted topiaries, especially the spiral forms, are chic and popular Christmastime decoratives, particularly for exterior display. But this hanging alternative, an inventive reinterpretation of the traditional sculpted composition, offers more flexibility, since it can not only adorn exterior doors, but it can grace interior spaces as well and can even be placed horizontally to bedeck doors, mirrors and mantels.

The spiraled swag, composed with a ready-made pine garland secured to a custom-crafted bamboo support, is embellished with a celestial collection of seasonal baubles and, appropriately, a few tufts of white *Viburnums*, commonly known as snowballs.

materials:
silk/permanent
  Viburnums
  permanent "fresh cut" pine garland
other
  iced stars
  glitter stars
  3-inch gold opal-finish glass balls
  3-inch moss matte-finish glass balls
  5-inch moss matte-finish glass balls
  burned bamboo
  green metallic wire

Star Light, Star Bright

Celestial tree toppers decorate elevated miniature pines.

1 Glue a small foam cylinder atop each candle-holder. Dip the tree "trunk" into pan-melt glue, and insert it into the foam.

2 Bend heavy-gauge wire into a hairpin shape. Cover the foam with moss, and secure the moss to the foam with the hairpin wires.

3 Wrap bead garland around the moss-covered foam, allowing the beaded tendrils to cascade from the candle plate.

Illustrative of the radiance of the star in the East that guided the wise men of old, these luminous twinkling stars top a pair of stemmed miniature pine trees, which are elevated atop amber glass ball candleholders. The stars' sparkling brilliance is continued in shimmering beaded garland "tree skirts," which glamorize the petite pines.

Ornamenting the trees like tiny glass balls are sprays of harvest-hued faux cranberries, chosen to reflect the golden amber of the candleholders. Sprigs of sweet anise, tucked among the diminutive boughs, fill out the airy branch configuration.

Sell these ritzy accents in pairs for décor and in multiples for holiday entertaining.

materials:
silk/permanent
  mini pine tree stems
  sweet anise
  cranberry picks
other
  crystal stars
  brown/amber bead garland
  moss
  dry foam
  pan-melt glue
  double ball candleholder
  triple ball candleholder

Jolly Gerberas

Holiday-enhanced *Gerberas* joyfully herald the Christmas season.

1 Bundle the *Gerberas* into a topiary. Insert them into the vase, and hold them upright. Wedge needle pine tightly around the *Gerbera* stems until the topiary can stand alone.

2 Enwrap a pine cone with a length of twig garland, tucking the vine under the cone's "shingles." Twist the garland to secure. Follow the same procedure for the second cone.

3 Attach the pine cones to the *Gerberas* by winding the twig vines around the florals' stems, just beneath the blossoms, which also secures them in the topiary form.

Sumptuous *Gerberas*, in a merry Christmas-red hue, are bundled into a topiarylike bouquet and accessorized for the holidays with lengthy strobus cone adornments that encircle the stems like nature's pendent jewels. Serving as the mechanic and holding the bundled *Gerbera* stems upright are boughs of needle pine, wedged tightly into the vase opening, further enhancing the topiary's seasonal appeal.

The pleasing arrangement, featuring popular but unconventional holiday florals, will display singly in entryways, bedrooms and other smaller spaces and will also make a grand impression in pairs on mantels, sidetables and other sizeable tabletops.

materials:
silk/permanent
   Gerberas
   needle pine
dried/preserved
   strobus cones
other
   twig garland
   brown vase

99

Modern Orb Trio

Traditional holiday hues are presented in unexpected materials.

1 Form a cluster of angel vine into a ball. Place a few permanent leaves onto the vine ball, and adhere leaves with wrappings of copper bullion wire. Add a few more leaves, and wrap with wire.

2 Clip yarrow stems to a uniform short length, and insert them into the plastic-foam sphere. Continue until the foam is covered with yarrow.

3 Enwrap the red yarrow-covered sphere with red bullion wire. Follow the same procedure to create the green yarrow orb, and repeat the wrapping technique using green bullion wire.

The conventional colors of Christmas are incorporated into this rather unconventional seasonal accent that offers an unexpected Euro-chic perspective using the ubiquitous holiday hues.

Resting in the basin of a shallow bowl, in a modern metallic finish, is a trio of orbs, two of which are colored yarrow amassed onto plastic-foam spheres. The other orb, adorned with fabric leaves and bound with copper bullion wire, is fashioned by hand from angel vine. Given a hint of sparkle by their metallic wire wrappings, the spheres decorate for the season in a thoroughly modern way. Use them on coffee tables, and adapt the concept to other seasons throughout the year.

materials:
dried/preserved
  yarrow
  angel vine
silk/permanent
  smilax leaves
other
  green wire
  copper bullion wire
  red bullion wire
  plastic-foam spheres
  bowl

Bejeweled Candle

Sparkling beads glamorize candlelit seasonal accessories.

1 Snip a holly spray into two pieces, and trim the excess stems, so the holly will fit in the container. Drop the holly into the vessel.

2 Apply a strip of florists' clay around the base of a candle. Place the candle into the holder, and gently press on the candle to secure it in place.

3 Wind the bead garlands around the base of the candle, allowing the beaded sprays to spill over the container's lip.

For a quick and easy offering during the busy Christmas season, without sacrificing the glitz and glamour typically associated with the holidays, enhance a pillar candle with shimmering bead garlands.

Here, a ribbed pillar candle is placed atop a clear glass holder that is filled with iconic berried holly. The glittering garlands, like a tinseled collar, surround the ruby pillar and attire the otherwise indistinctive accessory for even the most elegant affairs.

Create this design in coordinated multiples for holiday entertaining as well as basic seasonal home décor. And, if necessary, adapt it to other color schemes by changing the colors of the candle and garland.

materials:
silk/permanent
   berried holly
other
   bead garlands
   pillar candle
   florists' clay
   glass candleholder/vase

101

Berried Hedge

An opulent geometric topiary of uncomplicated construction.

1 Cut river cane to a uniform length. Insert it into a foam-filled container in a tight rectangular pattern, forming a hedge. Conceal the foam with reindeer moss.

2 Cut the pepperberry garland into sections. Dip the clipped stems into glue, and insert them into the tops of the river cane. Glue some stems between the canes as needed for a lush presentation.

3 Remove the loops used to hang the ornaments, and dip the hanging ends into glue. Nestle the ornaments among the berries in two offset rows, like a zigzag pattern. Cover the exposed glue with moss.

Whether greeting guests arriving for holiday gatherings or decorating extravagant buffets or other lavish spreads, this majestic berried topiary, whose lush fruits are jeweled, as a crown, with gleaming ornaments, will enchant guests with its powerful presence.

Despite its grand and stately airs, this dramatic topiary is unexpectedly easy to construct. The geometric mass of river cane, shaped to echo the old-world-inspired container, holds the pepperberry profusion in place; the berries' stems are simply glued into and among the hollow canes. Vibrant mounds of reindeer moss, surrounding the canes and the ornament finials, complement and enliven the muted sanguine palette.

materials:
dried/preserved
river cane
mood moss
reindeer moss
silk/permanent
pepperberry garland
other
red drop ornaments
plastic foam
pan-melt glue
rectangular planter

index

4
6
8
10
12
14
16
18
20
22
24
26
28
30
32
34
36
38
40
42
44
46
48
50
52
54
56
58
60
62
64
66
68
70
72
74
76
78
80
82
84
86
88
90
92
94
96
98

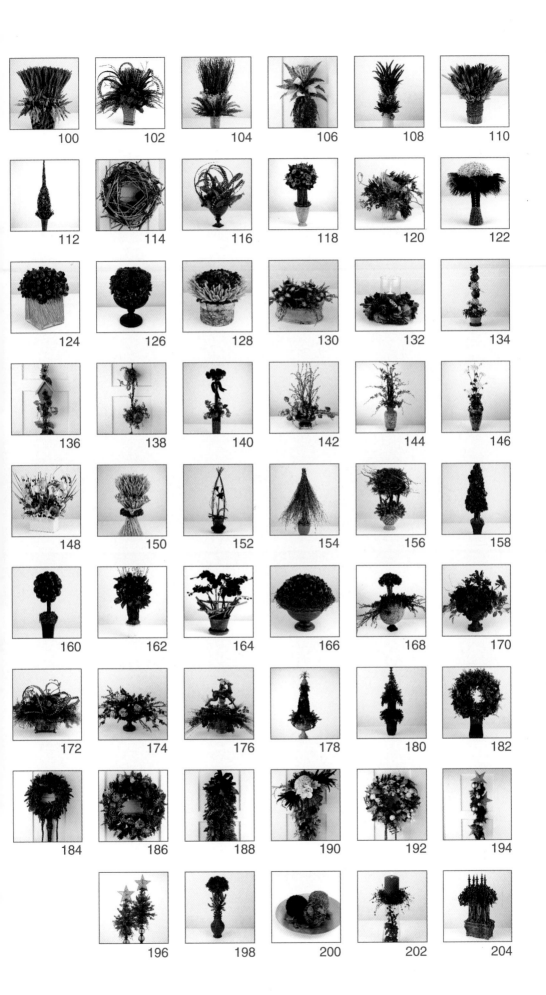

100   102   104   106   108   110

112   114   116   118   120   122

124   126   128   130   132   134

136   138   140   142   144   146

148   150   152   154   156   158

160   162   164   166   168   170

172   174   176   178   180   182

184   186   188   190   192   194

196   198   200   202   204